CHOPPERS

MIKE SEATE

MOTORBOOKS
INTERNATIONAL

This edition first published in 2003 by Motorbooks International, an imprint of MBI Publishing Company, Galtier Plaza, Suite 200, 380 Jackson Street, St. Paul, MN 55101-3885 USA

The information in this book is true and complete to the best of our knowledge. All recommendations are made without any guarantee on the part of the author or Publisher, who also disclaim any liability incurred in connection with the use of this data or specific details.

We recognize that some words, model names and designations, for example, mentioned herein are the property of the trademark holder. We use them for identification purposes only. This is not an official publication.

Motorbooks International titles are also available at discounts in bulk quantity for industrial or sales-promotional use. For details write to Special Sales Manager at Motorbooks International Wholesalers & Distributors, Galtier Plaza, Suite 200, 380 Jackson Street, St. Paul, MN 55101-3885 USA.

Library of Congress Cataloging-in-Publication Data available

ISBN 0-7603-1339-3

Cover photo credits:
Top front: *Guiseppe Roncen*
Bottom front: *Dain Gingerelli*
Back: *Dain Gingerelli*

Frontispiece: *Guiseppe Roncen*
Title Page: *Easyriders* magazine
On the back cover: *Dain Gingerelli*

Edited by Darwin Holmstrom
Designed by Tom Heffron

Printed in China

Contents

Acknowledgments

Photo by Kim Love

This book would still be, like many a project bike sitting in an unlit garage, just an unrealized vision if not for the people who, at no personal advantage, helped me get it on the road. King-sized thanks and much love to Darwin Holmstrom and Dain Gingerelli for guidance and being good friends and editors; Jesse (the Vanilla Gorilla) James; Dave Nichols at *Easyriders* magazine; Guiseppe Roncen, who can drop mad science on choppers all day long; Chopper Dave Freston for raiding his archives; Marilyn Stemp and *IronWorks* magazine; Mondo Porras at Denver's Choppers; Cindy Sparks and the crew at Hatton-Brown Publishing; and Paul Martinez, Butch Lassiter, Dave Perewitz, Lee Patterson, Vic Swnicki, Tommy Williams, and my wife, Kim Love.

Foreword
By Dave Nichols, Editor, Easyriders *magazine*

Blood, Sex, and Chrome

Some say that America's love affair with those spindly, savage, custom "murder-cycles" known as choppers began in 1947. World War II was over and returning flyboys were looking for the high-octane thrills that could only be found behind the chromed ape-hangers of a chopped Harley-Davidson.

What happened next has become a festering sore in the annals of motorcycling history. An incident occurred that single-handedly created an unwholesome image for Harley-Davidson motorcycles and those who ride them. There's no doubt that the image of the leather-clad hellion blasting down the road on a loud Harley, out to rape your daughters and sons, was invented due to some antisocial activities that took place at an American Motorcyclist Association (AMA) rally on July Fourth, 1947, in Hollister, California. Although much has been written about this "occurrence," little is truly known.

Dave Nichols

What is known is that Hollister hosted motorcycle races long before the alleged incident and still has a hell of a party in its humble burg, which includes biker activities (such as the 50th anniversary of the "incident" in 1997). As the story goes, World War II servicemen and flyers who were jaded by the war and used to white-knuckle thrills and excitement got into riding big chopped Harleys (known then and now as Hogs). They'd strip everything they could off of Harley dressers to make the bikes lighter. These "bobbers" became the forerunners to the "choppers" of the '60s and '70s.

The clean lines of a 1960s-era longbike characterize the customs built by Jesse James and company at West Coast Choppers. Guiseppe Roncen

Of the nearly 4,000 riders who came to watch the races at Hollister that fateful Independence Day, just a handful of guys belonged to the so-called "outlaw" clubs like the Boozefighters and Galloping Gooses. The misdemeanors that took place over the course of the weekend were pretty much of the "public intoxication" variety, but there happened to be a photographer from *Life* magazine who staged a few shots with a rather large fella posed on a Harley (not even *his* Harley, mind you) with a bunch of empty beer bottles artfully placed around the bike. The photographer went click, click, click, and in no time, the famous photo of the deadly drunken biker made its way to the cover of *Life* magazine and into the history books.

Almost overnight, motorcyclists became crazed, bloodthirsty bikers to the public at large. Lock your doors, guard your daughters, they're coming to your town! Always ready to cash in on a trend, Stanley Kramer pumped up America's dread for bikers with his 1954 release *The Wild One,* a Hollister-inspired work of fiction starring Marlon Brando and Lee Marvin. Brando rode a Harley in real life along with such contemporaries as Lee Marvin, Clark Gable, Robert Young, Errol Flynn, and Elvis Presley, but in the movie, Brando's character Johnny putts around on a Triumph while bad boy Lee Marvin gets the chopped Harley bobber.

The Wild One inspired a number of cheesy knock-off films (including Roger Corman's *Wild Angels*) and Harley's new 1957 XL Sportster in-spired America's youth to turn up the collars on their leather jackets and hit the highways, setting the stage for the 1960s.

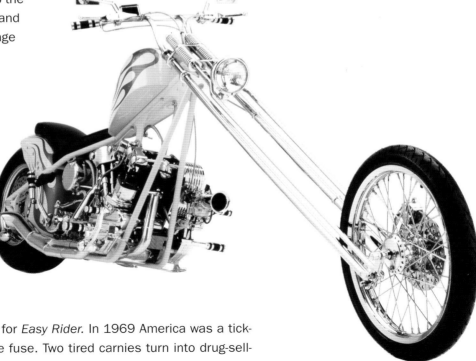

The turbulent '60s was a time of war and chaos. Timothy Leary was teaching us to "tune in, turn on, and drop out." It was a time of Vietnam, Kent State, Watergate, hippies, yippies, and Woodstock. What a long, strange trip it's been. Into this bubbling cultural stew came two maverick filmmakers with a vision. The timing was perfect for *Easy Rider.* In 1969 America was a ticking bomb and Peter Fonda lit the fuse. Two tired carnies turn into drug-selling bikers and become icons of America along the way. Captain America—with his red, white, and blue stars and stripes chopper—is the quiet reminder of what this country stands for. He is liberty. Dennis Hopper's Billy (as in Billy the Kid) is the ugly American, the frontiersman with his pushy

Denver's Choppers

Jesse James compromised on this bike a bit—it features a Softail-style rear suspension in place of the traditional hardtail frame—but given the fact James rode this bike to Sturgis, South Dakota, he should be allowed a bit of comfort.

Guiseppe Roncen

ways and rebellious spirit. They are America incarnate as they roll across this country looking for themselves. America sold out and so did the Captain and Billy. Despite the deeper meaning Fonda meant to capture in his film, American youth saw something else. They saw two free spirits on wild Harley choppers bein' gunned down by ignorant Southern rednecks. More than one teenager sewed an American flag on his jacket and went out and bought a bike that summer. Did you?

One thing is certain, by 1971 choppers were the rage. It was into this churning custom caldron of impossibly long front ends, rigid frames, stroked motors, wild "sissy bars," and handlebars that reached to the stars, that *Easyriders* magazine was unleashed on an unsuspecting public. Just as Fonda and Hopper's film *Easy Rider* acted as a microcosm of the hippie and biker culture, so *Easyriders* focused this wild lifestyle and defined it. Today,

A Paul Yaffee Original, right down to the upswept air cleaner on the S&S "E" series carburetor.

Paul Martinez

Introduction

Choppers
Forever!

In 1974, *Washington Post* writer Thierry Sangier claimed, "No one would ever write a book about choppers." The statement appeared in his book, *Bike!* which chronicled the state of motorcycling by the last quarter of the twentieth century. At the time, it may have been easy to dismiss choppers as yet another '60s generation fad, a pop culture artifact that would soon vanish faster than bell bottoms and DayGlo peace sign jewelry.

Sangier and many others in the motorcycling industry, however, weren't plugged into the deep, almost fanatical passion that chopped and customized motorcycles were inspiring in bikers around the globe. They didn't

A pretty girl, a chopper, and a party with a few hundred of your closest friends. What more do you need?

Guiseppi Roncen

Jesse James aboard the chopper he rode to Sturgis in the documentary **Motorcycle Mania II.** Guiseppe Roncen

see the desperate and truly inspired attempts to recreate movie choppers in tiny Swedish garages. They hadn't counted on a chopper parts aftermarket that continued to serve its core audience despite radical changes in custom motorcycles, and they surely didn't count on the emergence of today's highly talented, third-generation chopper builders.

Indian Larry works on his bike with the West Coast Choppers crew.

Guiseppe Roncen

You can't really blame the naysayers for expecting the chopper to fade from the motorcycling landscape. For most of the twentieth century, chopped motorcycles were an undeniable totem of streetwise rebellion, as easily linked to antisocial behavior as switchblade knives and regular visits to a parole officer. Much like the fast, flashy, and loud hotrod cars that had caused parents to panic in the early rock 'n' roll era of the 1950s, choppers presented Main Street America with a style in direct opposition to

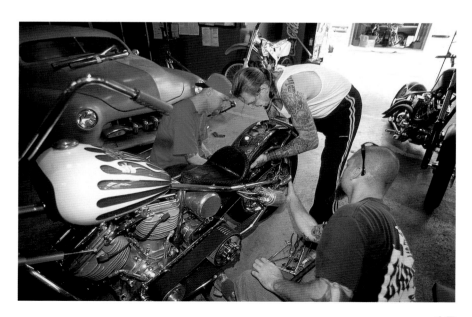

British expatriate Russ Mitchell's choppers are typical of British customs—black, raw, and mean.

Dain Gingerelli

Indian Larry, one of the East Coast's better-known chopper builders, on his rigid Panhead.

Guiseppi Roncen

everything the status quo held dear. Chopper riders weren't the "nicest people" you'd meet on a Honda, as the famous ad campaign declared, and they weren't interested in Electra Glide push-button starters, waterproof fiberglass saddlebags, or projecting an image that wouldn't offend the neighbors. They were and they remain outlaw machines, the sort of motorcycle that almost guarantees that your date's parents will worry when you drop your kickstand on their lawn and ask if their little girl is home.

As choppers spread with astonishing speed across America in the 1960s and early '70s, mainstream America fought back with an almost continuous wave of legislation, laws aimed directly at reining in the mechanical exuberance of a generation determined to express themselves with spray guns and welding torches.

Choppers, they reasoned, were about as in your face as a pair of brass knuckles, and for many, they were just about as frightening. When Sangier wrote *Bike!* back in 1974, he was correct in expecting that choppers would eventually be outlawed into submission, and he was nearly right. Some will

The popularity of choppers in Europe kept the breed alive when its popularity declined in the United States.

Guiseppi Roncen

say it was constant roadside harassment and impossible-to-pass state vehicle inspection laws that nearly killed the chopper, while others blame an increasingly clever motorcycle industry that co-opted the chopper's mechanical cool and made it safe and marketable.

The "fat bike" look of the 1990s and the emergence of the risk-free factory custom motorcycles—which had been designed not by a back-alley visionary mechanic but by corporate marketing research groups—both point to a motorcycle industry determined to co-opt some of the chopper's inherent cool without putting customers or themselves at risk.

So even as local police departments, federal safety organizations, and the corner motorcycle dealerships denounced—and, occasionally, harassed—chopper riders, the laid-back style and antiestablishment joie de vivre of riding a chopper were a two-wheeled Pandora's box that "The Man" couldn't stuff a cork in regardless of how hard he tried.

In the years since early chopper aficionados first stripped their motorcycles of excess baggage in a quest for improved speed and style, choppers have evolved beyond what even the most imaginative 1950s greaser could have imagined. Front forks grew to lengths that required the breadth of an aircraft carrier to turn and then, years later, contracted to more functional designs. Simple primer and spray-can finishes have evolved into fantastical murals, chemical finishes, and dazzling lacquer hues, dozens of coats deep.

Some things never go out of style. The timeless cool of the early chopper is recreated in this monochrome Evolution bobber.

Dain Gingerelli

Judging from the smile on the face of this lovely lass, it's not the length of the extension on your fork tube, but how you use it. Author's collection

Opposite page
During the original chopper craze, a home builder could get rigid chopper frames for just about any motorcycle engine, from a fire-breathing Harley-Davidson XLCH to a mild-mannered Honda CB350.

Author's collection

Comprised of equal parts baroque mechanical innovation and bad-ass street cred, the chopper, regardless of what motor powers it and what decade it was built in, has come to symbolize backstreet ingenuity at its most outrageous. Early rigid frames, revered for their almost military resilience and laid-back low profile, have become chrome moly engineering marvels with more elaborate twists and bends than a John le Carré novel.

No self-respecting chopper builder, from the lowliest backyard hacksaw surgeon to the big-bucks empires of Roger Bourget, Pat Kennedy, and Ron Simms, will launch a machine into the streets with a bone-stock motor; whopping aftermarket engines, boasting displacements and horsepower figures to rival modern sports cars, are now the norm, not the exception. Chopper riders have formed wildly complex bonds with their machines, personalizing them with illustrations of everything from political beliefs, to military histories, to gang and club affiliations, and even to bold sexual imagery.

You just don't see that kind of rider-bike interface with touring machines.

RIGID FRAMES.

LOOK FOR THE A.E.E. TRADEMARK STAMPED ON YOUR PARTS. IF IT'S NOT THERE IT'S NOT A.E.E.

WE SHIP BY PART NUMBERS ONLY. DOUBLE CHECK YOUR PART NUMBERS.

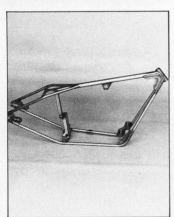

SPORTSTER RIGID FRAME

This all new construction frame is manufactured from special quality steel selected for the rigid requirements of street use. Frame was designed so that it accepts either kick or electric start engine with no alterations — easy bolt-on of stock components. This new construction rigid frame should meet state requirements where alterations or modifications are prohibited. AEE frame is 6 inches longer than the stock Sportster frame. Comes with a 10-degree neck angle change.

O-100 Frame . . . . **$275.00 ea.**

HONDA 450 RIGID FRAME

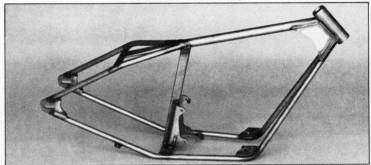

HONDA 350 RIGID FRAME

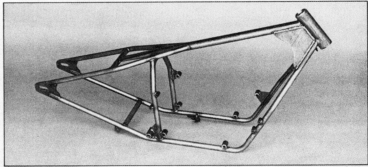

HONDA 750 RIGID FRAME
HONDA RIGID FRAMES

Now you can make a chopper from your Honda which will take on the appearance of the traditional chopper. These frames were designed with a 10-degree rake in the neck and a 6-inch increase in the overall length. You may use the components from your stock Honda which will bolt right into this frame. These new construction rigid frames should meet state requirements where alterations or modifications are prohibited. These frames are backed with the famous AEE guarantee.

O-102	Honda 450	. . . . . Frame	**$275.00 ea.**
O-103	Honda 350	. . . . . Frame	**$275.00 ea.**
O-105	Honda 750	. . . . . Frame	**$275.00 ea.**

Angular Z-Bars, whitewall tire, and Morris magneto ignition are '60s staples, but this bike was built in the year 2000.

Guiseppi Roncen

Radical posture and serious detailing mark this Italian Shovelhead chopper.

Guiseppi Roncen

Chopper Dave in the process of turning back the clock.

Guiseppe Roncen

Some credit the aging Baby Boomer generation with resurrecting the chopper, while others attribute the chopper's return, more appropriately, to the custom bike explosion happening overseas. Die-hard chopper fanatics will tell you the longbike never went out of style, while still others ascribe the chopper's newfound celebrity status to an energetic group of latter-day

chopper builders. Men like Jesse James, Billy Lane, and Mike Maldonado have taken the outrageous longbike concepts of the 1960s and turned them into high-dollar, high-concept rolling sculptures.

Despite the chopper's ascent from the outlaw fringes of motorcycling to the designer-label, image-conscious streets of the twenty-first century, choppers continue to play the same role in motorcycling they always have: They're eye candy that rolls; a type of motorcycle that, in style and substance, permanently has its middle finger raised toward convention and conformity.

During a late 1990s visit to the United States, a representative from Italy's Bimota Motor Corporation, builders of handmade supersport motorcycles, observed a group of American bikers ignoring a display of his firm's technologically complex machines while streaming straight for a rickety old Harley-Davidson Knucklehead chopper parked nearby.

"Why would anyone take a perfectly good, stock motorcycle and take off the shocks and mufflers, alter the steering geometry so that it handles less sharply?" he asked in heavily accented English. That question has been asked thousands of times before by chopper nonbelievers, and similar inquiries have surrounded the chopper like mid-pack exhaust fumes. In these pages, we'll attempt to illustrate and answer that intangible question and, along the way, capture some of the flash, some of the laid-back style, and some of the bad-boy fun that are an integral part of every chopper on the road.

The umlauts on that road sign indicate this American-style chopper is a long way from America. Guiseppe Roncen

Chapter 1

From Bombers to Bobbers

The Origins and Early Days of the Chopper

Consider the brakeless front end of the stretch chopper era. When '60s-era chopper designers raised the ire of the safety community by lopping off or disconnecting front brake linkages in order to shun safety as uncool and un-clutter their motorcycle's lines, they were actually emulating the early bobbers who frequently eschewed their front brakes for more practical reasons. Race bikes from flat trackers to hill climb machines didn't need front brakes be-cause these types of purpose-built motorcycles only needed to go faster, not slow down. And anyway, those early drum hubs were damn heavy. They weighed enough to slow a motorcycle down, so they often found themselves on the scrap heap alongside front fenders, horns, lights, and, in some cases, a bike's protective primary chain cover.

And those slick-looking billet aluminum, side-mounted taillight and license plate holders that sell for $400 today? Well, mounting a license tag on a side frame rail—to confuse the odd perusing cop—was a clever innovation created by the "bob job" bikers nearly 60 years ago.

Of course, most motorcyclists declined to chop parts off, or bob, their mo-torcycles in the pre- or immediate post-WWII period. In fact, most American motorcyclists riding bikes with rigid rear suspension preferred newfangled technological advances like densely-padded sprung seats, weather-resistant Plexiglas windshields, and (relatively) quiet exhaust systems. These were the

Before helmet laws and years before authorities began targeting choppers for safety violations, the early '60s were a chopper rider's paradise.

Dain Gingerelli

days when lower back problems were as common to motorcyclists as hemorrhoids. Days when kidney belts—thick, rawhide lumbar support garments entirely necessary for long rides on a ground-pounding rigid bike—were a part of any serious enthusiast's riding gear. Most bikers utilized their mounts as primary transportation in those days, so a family's two-wheeler could very easily find itself hauling the groceries home on Saturday, crossing the state to visit relatives on Sunday, or maybe blasting down a dirt path for an impromptu hare and hound race with some friends during a summer outing. With motorcycles pressed into multiple-use service, keeping a machine practical and comfortable was a primary concern for most riders.

And though it would be a few years before news of drunken motorcyclists invading sleepy Hollister, California, crept into the headlines, forever marking the bobber riders as a public menace, many, if not most, motorcyclists were preoccupied with maintaining an acceptable image. Conformity ruled not only the dynam-

In addition to the Maltese-cross mirror, this Harley Sportster-based chopper, named "The Hustler," features ignition switches in a molded-in dash compartment. Dain Gingerelli

ics of biking; it manifested itself in everything from rider's apparel to roadway travel. Most motorcycle shops in the 1940s and '50s sponsored brand-specific clubs for their customers; in nearly every instance, those clubs wore distinct uniforms, color-coordinated paramilitary-style clothes designed to create a group identity for riding clubs.

By today's standards, these jaunty fashions, with broad, pinstriped jodhpurs, saddle shoes, rodeo-style shirts, and tastefully embroidered insignias, appear to have rolled out of a drum and baton corps catalog. But to riders in mid-twentieth century America, many of whom had suffered during the Great Depression, the garb represented a source of endless pride and, like the motorcycle itself, a means of escape from the drudgery of everyday responsibilities and blue-collar jobs. Similarly, the motorcycles from this era followed a strict mechanical regimentation: Riders mainly stuck with the conservative paint schemes and performance of their stock bikes, while accouterments were limited, mostly, to elaborate sheepskin seat covers, a shifter knob in the

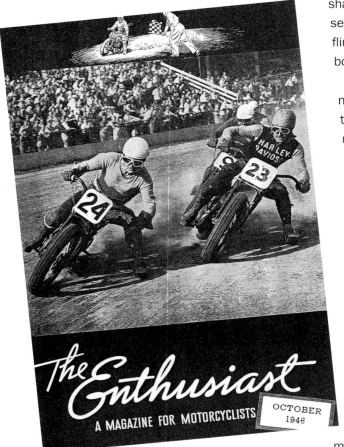

shape of a gaming die or piston, and maybe, just maybe, a set of wider-than-stock handlebars. In this climate of stifling conformity, it's amazing that, as a subculture, the bobber/chopper movement survived at all.

But for many bikers, the factory's motorcycle was nothing more than a good reference point, a decent place to start building your own vision of two-wheeled excitement. Born partly out of the necessity for improved performance and partly out of the motorcyclist's unyielding need for individuality and self-expression, the chopper crowd slowly emerged as the AMA club's opposite number. By the time millions of returning servicemen began choosing motorcycles both as a means of cheap transportation and a way to blow off some serious postwar angst, there was already a cultural division between the strictly regulated "straight" motorcycle clubs and riders of customized bikes.

Many of the early bob job riders were servicemen returning from as much as a half-decade overseas in uniform. They came home changed men, many of them looking to replicate some of the thrills and visceral danger of wartime life, and with a little money and a few nights in the garage, they could create machines that reminded them of the supercharged fighter planes and rugged military bikes they'd come to rely on in battle.

In time, they haphazardly developed a distinct uniform to match their minimalist bikes.

Along with the loud, often homemade bikes, barely legal with their tiny, magneto-powered lighting systems or running none at all, the early chopper riders favored the slouchy, dashing insouciance of the fighter pilot. They wore tall leather boots and military surplus leather A2 flight jackets. Many old time bobbers will tell you that drinking and raising hell were almost as important as riding itself. This presented a stark contrast to the parade-ground discipline of American Motorcyclists Association clubs. You'd be hard-pressed to locate a photo of a bob job rider from these early years without the ever-present beer bottle in hand. Their fierce appetite for the party life was reflected in the names of early chopper clubs such as California's Boozefighters, Coffin Cheaters, and 13 Rebels.

With vehicle design codes spottily enforced at best, many early chopper builders took full advantage of loopholes in the law; some deleted lighting systems altogether, while others adopted high-performance engine upgrades such as boring and restroking engines for bigger displacement and more horsepower—hop-ups proven while drag racing on the dry lake beds of Southern California. Repairing aircraft engines and refitting battle-damaged jeeps, trucks, and tanks made for some remarkably inventive postwar mechanics,

In the early days of bobbers and choppers, mainstream motorcycle publications like Harley's Enthusiast *refused to recognize the custom bike movement.* Author's collection

many of whom, like Wisconsin's George Smith, put his military skills to use in the early motorcycle performance scene, producing drag racing engines and, later, engine upgrade kits under the S&S Cycle label. In the past half-century, the specifics of chopper building are as removed from these early, raw-performance Hogs as a Pentium processor is from an Underwood manual typewriter. Still, it is worth noting the timeworn modifications that still hold up today.

Flywheels on the big 80 cubic inchers were frequently shaved in machine shops to lighten their throw during high-revving drag strip launches. Larger-diameter carburetors were adapted from any available source. Some, like the bell-domed S.U., were salvaged from the engines of

With his leather aviator's helmet, equestrian jodphurs, and tall boots, biker Gene Probst looks ready to pilot a bi-plane as he mounts his 1939 Harley Flathead. Fringed "buddy" seat, windshields, and saddlebags were de-rigueur in the pre-chopper period.
Lee Patterson collection

Eight-year-old Lee Probst-Patterson poses on her father's brand-new 1941 Harley-Davidson side-valve Flathead. Family riding groups mounted on pristine touring bikes would soon be eclipsed by chopper clubs with an entirely different aesthetic. Lee Patterson collection

imported cars to increase combustion. Some ingenious tuners even adopted dual manifolds allowing second carburetors to run simultaneously. Engine heads were ported and polished for a smoothness that would impress a jeweler in order to hasten that all-important flow of exhaust gases from the top end. Horsepower, light weight, and speed were the rule, and many mechanics from the bobber era, working on shoestring budgets, attained quarter-mile records that stood at California drag strips well into the 1970s.

Along with hot rodders who more often than not drag raced their souped-up jalopies on public roads, the riders of highly customized bobber bikes were rapidly developing a reputation as outlaws. Many late-night drag races ended in a squeal of tires and the wail of a police siren. There seemed to be a couple of fast bikers in every town, and eventually they found each other at a red light. In an interview published in *Easyriders* magazine in 1983, early street racer and

bob job pioneer "Wino" Willie Forkner recalled that street racers organized field meets where they could trade go-fast secrets and customizing tricks.

Forkner said it was not unusual for bikers to ride all day to a race, tear all of the auxiliary lighting from their bikes, compete in a race, and then bolt everything back on in order to make it to that evening's beer blast. "We did things like fall out of windows and race down the middle of the street, but we did 'em in innocence. When a Boozefighters member would fall asleep at a campground, we'd pour a circle of gas around him and his bike and light it. That woke 'em up fast, but we never hurt anybody, because we'd all been hurt in the war, believe me, baby. All of us had suffered in that war."

The vets may have suffered for their country, but the AMA was having none of its extended post-war celebration. Members of clubs like the Boozefighters were commonly ostracized for their throttle-happy, beer-fueled antics, and an atmosphere of "Oh no, here they come again" started to precede the bob job riders as faithfully as a highway patrol car.

The two camps would become forever polarized just two years after WWII ended, in the small town of Hollister, California. During the town's annual Fourth of July Gypsy Tour and Races, mischief, testosterone, and plenty of wide-open throttles created the first "motorcycle riot" and, subsequently, helped spread an entire culture of two-wheeled rebellion. Much has been written about the actual events of that Fourth of July weekend, a gathering that in recent years has taken on the mythic proportions of the Watts Riots or Tianamen Square's democracy protests. Bikers who actually attended the 1947 Hollister Rally claim that the drunken, amateur stunt shows and main street drag races that caused the locals to call in the sheriff's department and highway patrol were too innocent and harmless to be described as a genuine riot.

Before his death in 1989, Forkner claimed that errant bikers actually paid for whatever saloon windows and barroom interiors had been damaged in the

various brawls that transpired at Hollister. Likewise, most of the 4,000 bikers who "took over the town" were only perceived to have done so because there were so few hotel rooms available that many simply slept on neighborhood lawns. But in a desperate attempt to distance themselves from the subsequent public relations scandal that followed motorcycling after Hollister, the AMA made the infamous declaration that "99 percent of all motorcyclists are decent law-abiding citizens," unintentionally granting those choosing to identify with the "other" 1 percent a badge of infamy.

"Back in those days, 'outlaw' meant non-AMA, not a criminal gang," Forkner once told an interviewer. His is an important distinction as the term "outlaw" was then associated with bikers who drank hard and rode customized motorcycles. It would take another generation for the term "outlaw biker" to develop an entirely different and much more nefarious connotation. However, in the late 1940s and early '50s, a number of Harley and Indian riders quickly rallied around the label, further polarizing motorcyclists into opposing camps. Caught between their corporate masters and the needs of an increasingly diverse clientele, many Harley-Davidson and Indian motorcycle dealerships were forced to choose between their traditional, family-oriented customers and the sneering, leather-jacketed "outlaws" who were commonly seen astride machines that were anything but stock.

It took Hollywood only seven years to turn the Hollister rally into a motion picture. **The Wild One,** *starring a brawling Marlon Brando aboard a Triumph Thunderbird and Lee Marvin riding a bobbed Harley, was the first true outlaw biker epic.*

Author's collection

Many chose the former, with a lot of help from the media.

As the Hollister story was enhanced and exaggerated with Hollywood's release of *The Wild One* in 1954, the image of the outlaw biker was firmly implanted in the public's consciousness. Film buffs and chopper fans alike have questioned how Marlon Brando's portrayal of the mumbling leader of the Black Rebels Motorcycle Club could have contributed so much to the chopper culture. True, Brando's stock Triumph Thunderbird looked like the sort of motorcycle favored by algebra teachers with particularly healthy adventure streaks. It was the clapped-out, primer-covered Harley ridden by his film rival Chino, played to drunken perfection by a young Lee Marvin, that more accurately

embodied the minimalist bob-bers of the era. Nevertheless, it was Brando's unforgettably anti-establishment attitude and his laid-back resistance to anything that smacked of middle-class re-spectability and social conformi-ty that made his *Wild One,* the literal poster child for the nas-cent chopper movement.

While Brando and, a few years later, a Memphis truck driver named Elvis Presley bus-ied themselves making pouty lips and greasy hair popular with rebels everywhere, the British motorcycle industry was

Little Joe and friends chilling out in Burbank before a ride. Ape-hanger handlebars and sissy-bar backrests were, in the late 1950s, being manufactured from found materials including bar-stool legs and cannibalized kitchen chairs. Dave Freston

doing its own number on the bob job scene. Since its introduction in 1938, Triumph's Speed Twin, a nimble, 365-pound, 500cc road burner, had been capable of besting anything from American manufacturers on race circuits and streets alike. By the mid-1950s, American motorcyclists were clamor-ing for speedy midsize machines from British manufacturers, including Nor-ton, BSA, and Ariel. Bone stock from the packing crate, Britain's latest mo-torcycles could achieve the sorts of triple-digit speeds that American bik-ers had busted many a knuckle trying to wrest out of their considerably heavier Harleys and Indians. These two manufacturing giants had been the only domestic motorcycle companies to emerge from the Great Depression

Atlantic City, New Jersey's, Jersey Devils motorcycle club, circa late 1950s. Custom motorcycles were still somewhat practical in these days, so radically raked and extended forks were still years from reality. Hacksaw-cut fenders and tall handlebars were the norm. Author's collection

with their assembly lines still humming. A few years of prosperity, mainly attributable to lucrative contracts supplying motorcycles to the military, almost ensured their survival—that is, until faced with the challenge of the British invasion.

Just as Harley-Davidson's owners would seek federal protection from lower-cost, high-performance Japanese motorcycles in 1984, the Milwaukee factory hired attorney Martin Paulsen to petition the U.S. Tariff Commission in 1952 on Harley's behalf. After two years of watching the British manufacturers whittle away at their market share, the Harley-Davidson Motor Company requested that the Feds hike import duties on British bikes from 10 to 40 percent. No way, said Uncle Sam—let the free market decide.

Unfortunately for Harley's sake, its traditional buyer base was deciding to ride British in record numbers. In 1950 Triumph brought in just over 1,000 of its 350cc and 500cc motorcycles. By 1960 Triumph was exporting some 9,000 of its tastefully styled, lightweight machines to the United States. By capturing all the important racing titles from Sacramento's flat tracks to Daytona's 200, the Brits were winning over the editors of even the most staunchly patriotic stateside enthusiast magazines. Costing hundreds less and weighing about one-third less than a Harley-Davidson Panhead FLH (Indian had gone belly up by this time), the British bikes were starting to make American motorcycles look pretty bad in comparison.

Despite all of the media hype surrounding the British invasion, a backlash was forming. Somewhere out there on the back roads and blasting down the main streets was a dedicated clientele for the American bikes, riders who were unimpressed with quarter-mile times, modern telescopic forks, hydraulic rear suspension units, and those effete, gentlemanly little bikes from Great Britain. These riders had grown attached to riding highly personalized machines, motorcycles that reflected not the mass-market appeal decided upon in corporate boardrooms but what an individual rider wanted from his bike. They wanted to be noticed for doing things differently from the next guy and wanted to be sure that, at even the largest biker gatherings, their motorcycle wouldn't be mistaken for anybody else's. They wanted to be noticed riding up the boulevard, wanted to reflect a savoir faire that was all but invisible in the stifling conformity of Eisenhower's America.

What they seemed to want was a chopper, and if the rest of the world didn't understand, well, all the better.

It was only natural that the chopper scene began to distance itself from the purely performance-oriented side of the bob job movement. The British bikes offered plenty of thrills for competition-oriented riders looking to prove their mettle on the sanctioned racetracks, drag strips, and dry lake beds. Many of the ace mechanics and tuners of the immediate post-WWII period were, by the late 1950s and early 1960s, operating speed shops servicing and selling British bikes. But to a growing number of hotheaded youngsters and old school Boozefighters alike, riding wasn't about burning up their machines in a constant game of one-upmanship. It was about looking and being cool, unhurried, and laid-back; the chopper, unlike the bobber, was coming to represent a blatant

Though Triumph marketed its sporty twins to performance enthusiasts, many ended up like this cool Tiger 650 custom. "Scalloped" paint on the peanut gas tank was by Von Dutch, legendary California pinstripe artist and custom motorcycle visionary. Dave Freston

display of mechanical and social irreverence in a country seemingly dedicated to working itself to death.

The rock 'n' roll aesthetic, which had burst on the scene offending and alarming many of the same elements of society that hated loud, flashy motorbikes, only added a crazy-cool soundtrack to the newfound outlaw biker culture; a sleek, stripped-down motorcycle, all big engine and attitude, was the perfect two-wheeled complement to a culture of hot rods and D.A. haircuts, of black leather and antisocial posturing. "Garbage wagons" and "sissy bikes," the greasers and chopper riders called the full-dressers and British sportsters, creating yet another cultural and aesthetic chasm in motorcycling. Just as the family motorcycle clubs and the bobbers had resented each other in the post-WWII era, the chopper riders, as the bobbers had come to be known by the early 1960s, felt themselves separate and different from all other motorcyclists.

Building a chopper back in those days wasn't easy. Just as the bobbers had found, there were no stocks of ready-made, aftermarket performance accessories waiting to be bolted on to their machines; the chopper builders had to make do with what they had or, more importantly, could make. Around 1960, when the California chopper culture was just emerging from a thousand back-alley garages and smoky machine shops, there was still no Paughco or Arlen Ness, no AEE bike-in-a-box, and no lavishly illustrated *Jammer's Handbook*.

Instead, when riders like Hell's Angels president and author Sonny Barger wanted a front fork for his 1936 Knucklehead that looked cooler and attracted more attention, he simply took a stock Harley-Davidson XA springer fork and cut a couple of inches from the rails. The same was done to another set, and then a third. With some skillful welding and a little luck, these early customizers fashioned the first extended front ends, a signature piece of any chopper. Likewise, in his 2000 biography *Hell's Angel*, Barger details how, in 1959, as an 18-year-old Army private, he fashioned a fast, unique-looking chopper from the well-used Knuckle, improvising and handcrafting whatever parts his bike needed from scratch. "For the quick take-off as well, we put in new cams and solid push rods, installed bigger valves and new pistons, punched out the carburetor and put close-ratio gears in the transmissions with bigger sprockets to make our motorcycles accelerate faster," Barger writes in his autobiography. It's much the same process that European chopper builders would follow in the '70s, when the movie *Easy Rider* helped spread the longbike gospel across that continent.

In 1959, when a group of Burbank riders posed for this pre-ride photo, the custom parts on their Triumph Bonnevilles and Harley-Davidson Panheads and Knuckleheads were all hand-made originals.

Dave Freston collection

Where parts shelves failed, imagination sufficed: Chopper builders would spend long nights dreaming up everything from elaborately sculpted sissy bar passenger backrests to methods of adapting smaller, shapelier gas tanks from Cushman and Mustang scooters to their Hogs.

"You've got to remember that bobbers didn't have extended front ends. The builders would either turn the front fender around and put it on the back wheel, or cut the original (hinged FLH) fender off at the hinge. Dog bone risers were popular to elevate a rider's hands and they'd put a Bates solo seat on the bike or dual carbs because the whole idea was to hop-up the bike, to make it faster," said master Harley-Davidson customizer Arlen Ness, who would later make his fortune and reputation in the chopper building fad that captured the San Francisco Bay Area in the late 1960s.

Getting his start at roughly the same time in South Dakota was Denny Berg, a fledgling chopper craftsman who today lends his formidable skills to building custom motorcycles for celebrities and major aftermarket parts corporations. Berg still fabricates most of the one-off parts that characterize his clean, well-proportioned choppers, a habit he picked up while growing up on a Midwestern ranch. Building choppers was easy for Berg and his biking buddies. They could turn a set of backup lights from a Volkswagen into chopper headlamps. They possessed the ability to rework fenders from an abandoned Ford pickup into custom fenders for a Panhead chopper. "We only had five, maybe six months of riding time. We had a lot of downtime to customize. I grew up on a ranch

With mainstream motorcycle magazines enforcing a blackout on chopped bikes, custom car shows, like this one held in Oakland, California, provided builders with much-needed creative outlets, even if it meant displaying their iron on a bed of mohair. Dave Freston

Despite the liberal application of chrome, hand-fabricated parts, and metal-flake paint, customs like "The Armenian," a rigid Harley-Davidson Knucklehead chopper, were most likely ridden on the streets. Note the skinny tires, cafe-style fork gaiters, and white leather seat—very cool!

Dave Freston

in the middle of nowhere, so I just learned how to fix things and build things with what we had lying around," he told *Cycle World* magazine in 1996.

The peaked chrome footrests, the highway peg and forward control, all came of age in the do-it-yourself era of the early 1960s. Forward foot controls that allow an extremely laid-back riding position came about almost by accident, according to Mondo Porras, a longtime chopper builder at Denver's Choppers in Henderson, Nevada. "Bikers noticed how the stock foot control position for Harley-Davidson FLH police models, with the out-front floorboards, when matched to the seating position on a rigid frame chopper, allowed them to kick their boots way out front and still reach the brakes. If you took off the floorboards and set a pair of pegs up there, it looked like they were sitting in a recliner while rolling down the highway," he recalled. This riding style, right out of the La-Z-Boy catalog, was soon the look to have, and Porras could barely keep up with the demand for parts. King and queen seats came about, early builders say, after too many female passengers complained that the new laid-back riding styles left them little, if any, back support. Up went a sissy bar tall enough to support Her Highness generously, and upholstering the bar to match the rest of the bike was simply a matter of time.

Porras said the craze for long, extended springer front ends started when bobbers would cut and weld "a couple of inches" into a set of steel girder forks from an old Indian, or a Harley-Davidson XA springer, to make their bikes handle better under rapid, straight line acceleration. "At first it was all about making your bike run and look like a drag bike, like the ones they raced out at El Mirage or Bonneville," Porras recalled. However, by 1965, customers were pouring into Denver's asking for longer and longer front forks for their choppers. At the time, no aftermarket existed for extended stock-replacement fork tubes to fit Harley-Davidson Sportster or British bike forks. Instead, builders looted old parts stashes for springer front forks, which were cheap and plentiful at the time. The Denver's team found an unlikely source for chopper parts in the axle struts from the frames of old Ford Model A's. In a rare coincidence of engineering, the Ford suspension parts were a perfect match in gauge, contour, and diameter to a

A man's prized possessions: a pretty bike and an even prettier woman. Harley's EL overhead-valve Knucklehead was the engine of choice for early customizers. Larger "stroker" flywheels and overbore pistons could be adapted from 80-cubic-inch Flathead models, and big-bore carbs yielded serious horsepower gains. Dave Freston

set of Harley-Davidson springer forks: Denver's worked up a jig that allowed sections as long as 24" to be welded into the motorcycle forks, creating what was arguably the first mass-produced aftermarket chopper front ends.

"They were damned heavy to steer, but we couldn't chrome them fast enough," Porras said.

It was a time of incredible innovation and found function for custom bike builders. Everything from cars to farm machinery to household appliances were studied and stripped down for use on choppers. Northern Californian Miller Blair remembers staring at automobile leaf springs and wondering to himself whether they could be transformed into parts for a chopper. A few years later, some determined welder fashioned that very item into a very long and flexible front end for a chopper. "Just about anything was fair game back in those days. If it could be welded, painted, or chromed, it was on a chopper," he said.

Just as everyday motorcyclists were in no big rush to trade in their FLH touring bikes for bobbers in the 1940s and '50s, the chopper trend, however popular on the West Coast, took its time spreading across the country. Celebrated documentary photographer Danny Lyon, who offered one of the first chronicles of the early outlaw biker scene in his 1966 pictorial *The Bikeriders*, claimed that choppers weren't exactly considered cool by the Chicago-area

"Is that a 12-inch extension or are you just happy to see me?" Can you say, "Phallic symbol"?

Guiseppe Roncon

Extending a set of stock Harley-Davidson XA springer forks was easy for the inventive early chopper builder. Sections of junked forks could be cut and welded in until the desired length was achieved. Dain Gingerelli

outlaws he rode with, at a time when West Coast builders like Blair, who later formed custom outfitter Jammer Enterprises, were already doing a brisk trade in handmade chopper parts. "The Outlaws used to make fun of bikes that were wildly painted with little tanks and stuff. They used to laugh about them running out of gas and that they really couldn't go anywhere," Lyon said.

Lyon's photos from this period clearly bear out this observation. In his most famous black and white print from his biker era, "Crossing the Ohio River," a member of the Kentucky Outlaws motorcycle club roars across a bridge span on what would today be accurately described as a rat bike; his weather-beaten Harley-Davidson Panhead sports a pair of chromed flat fenders riding close on the narrow white-wall tires, foot pegs bolted into the floorboard mounts for makeshift forward controls and a finish of dirty white paint on the Fat Bob gas tanks. A jockey-shift is clearly in place while the exhaust system is a homemade collector system that mounts up high in the manner of an XLCH Sportster's off-road pipe (further evidence of the influence of racing accessories on the bobbers and early choppers.) The forks appear to be stock-length FLH models, their only concessions to style being a set of rubber fork-tube gaiters and a replica of a Spanish Conquistador's helmet mounted atop the headlight.

This photo, like all of Lyon's work in *The Bikeriders* was taken between 1963 and 1967 and reveals how deeply entrenched the bobber look was on the outlaw psyche even then. A few of the bikes in Lyon's book are basically stock Triumph Bonnevilles sporting ape-hanger handlebars, while frequently these youngish, pompadoured riders can be seen riding stock Harley-Davidson Sportsters. Even these bikes, considered Milwaukee's lightweight, more modern answer to the British speedsters, remain in relatively stock trim, their only custom work being white rubber hand-grips or the odd Maltese cross painted on a gas tank. Though some very early choppers were surfacing in East Coast towns including New York and Boston in the early 1960s, the trend was almost exclusively a Southern California invention. This was, after all, the state where far-out custom concept cars had been designed by Ed "Big Daddy" Roth and George Barris, futuristic and almost cartoonish creations that captured many a youthful imagination. Thousands of motorcyclists had seen the custom cars and envisioned similar mechanical artistry bestowed on their two-wheelers. There were other factors

at play as well: Endless summers and a large, restless youth population with plenty of disposable income provided a perfect incubator for the chopper explosion that was about to unfold.

There's little wonder that choppers were slow to make their way across the country. Being long, low, and better when ridden in a straight line than slaloming through the bends, choppers are also a natural reflection of Southern California, an environment that features lots of long, straight roads. "Los Angeles is so flat, you can watch a thief steal your bike for three days," was a popular joke with chopper riders at the time. Some academics, including *Washington Post* writer Thierry Sangier, have traced the chopper's origins not to California's warm climate but to the brisk trade in stolen motorcycle parts in and around Southern California. "Motorcycles, beginning to be a common sight among West Coasters, were often stolen by motorcycle gang members for quick money. The bikes, once transported to a secret workshop, were made radically different, largely unrecognizable to former owners and peddled by fences for reduced prices," Sangier wrote in 1974.

There is some truth in this account. Mexico is only a few hours to the south of L.A., and a bike ridden across the border can easily disappear into a backstreet motorcycle garage, never to be seen again. Also, the practice of

Low in the back, high in the front, and cool all over describes this retro Bobber Panhead owned by Dave Freston of Burbank, California. Shotgun drag pipes, flat-tracker tires, and missing front fender are period-perfect, though the S&S Super Carb is a more modern touch. Dain Gingerelli

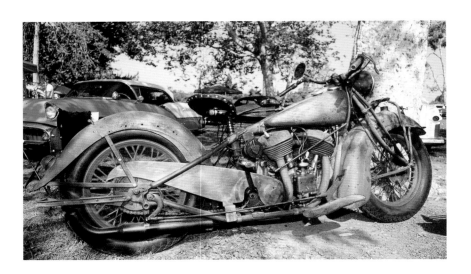

Even the faux-rust finish looks authentic on this twenty-first century recreation of an authentic Indian bobber!

Dain Gingerelli

Testament to the longevity of Indian motorcycles, this bobbed Chief is still up and running strong nearly 50 years after the last new V-twin motorcycle rolled out of the Springfield, Massachusetts, plant. Extended forks and shortened rear mudguard are courtesy of the owner. Dain Gingerelli

completely dismantling a motorcycle's engine during a chopper project invariably involves removing or splitting the engine cases. Because manufacturers stamp a motorcycle's all-important identifying serial numbers into the cases, tearing down an engine could provide a dodgy mechanic with the perfect excuse to erase or alter a motorcycle's identity. Imaginative machinists who know their way around a chisel and a DMV form could easily turn a set of stock Harley-Davidson Shovelhead's engine cases into the basis for a Pan-Shovel combo, complete with "authentic" serial numbers from a bike built many years previously. Change the stock five-gallon Fat Bob gas tanks for a narrow four-gallon Mustang unit, cut and reweld the frame neck for different rake and trail dimensions, and add a kicked-out 12-inch-over-stock set of forks, and this reborn bike is capable of passing even the most stringent state inspection.

Even the term "chopping" is indelibly related to the automobile chop shop where stolen cars are given new leases on life by shade-tree mechanics. Some of the first chopper stories to surface in the press involved elaborate, interstate motorcycle theft rings run by outlaw bike clubs. It was one of these very newspaper headlines—a stolen chopper caper gone wrong—that provided the basis for the 1966 Roger Corman biker classic *The Wild Angels.* Incidents like these may have been far from endemic in reality, but they further cemented in the public's mind a link between choppers and lawbreaking.

While lurid news stories about choppers made for thrilling headlines, they were just another headache for the gearheads and welding-torch artists who built and rode them. It didn't take long for many Harley-Davidson dealerships to adopt an informal policy of refusing to sell parts to chopper riders. And there were more than a few restaurants, hotels, and bars that felt it was their patriotic duty to turn away any youngster with the gall to turn up on one of those weird, chopped "motorsickles."

But all of that didn't matter to some. For rebellious American bikers in the early 1960s, a self-fabricated chopper was not only a source of endless tinkering and self-reinvention but a statement in

51

Previous page

An update on the vintage bobber, Italian style. Shoulder-high dice-topped shifter, tiny rear bobtail fender, and bare steel tractor seat are over-the-top fun. Guiseppi Roncen

A new generation of customizers like Jesse James of West Coast Choppers have kept the chopper alive into the twenty-first century.

Guiseppi Roncen

West Coast Choppers combines traditional chopper style with a postindustrial gutter punk aesthetic to create a unique take on an old genre.

Guiseppi Roncen

good old-fashioned can-do. For instance, early "ape-hanger" handlebars were sometimes fashioned out of the steel legs of kitchen chairs or bar stools. Chopper builders had to be skilled bodymen in order to apply precision layers of putty to "mold" frames, gas tanks, and fenders; they had to be consummate mechanics to keep their motors tuned and running, and they needed a keen eye for creating the next wild look that everyone else would envy.

The chopper was also coming to represent a weird and uniquely American backlash against the engineering comforts of the postwar economic boom. When Harley-Davidson replaced the ancient hand-shift "suicide clutches" on their Big Twins with easy-to-operate foot shifters in the 1950s, hard-core chopper builders defiantly sought out the difficult-to-control setups

and adopted them to custom bikes. Considered revolutionary when introduced in 1949, the patented Hydra Glide hydraulic forks gave a smoother
ride at all speeds; chopper builders said no thanks—give us the old, un-
damped springer forks, and you can stuff the spacious saddlebags and
roomy saddles too.

The desired end result of these toolshed customs, was, of course,
maximum visibility. In this chopper riders were more than successful.
Where hot-rodders were once doggedly targeted by law enforcement, it was
now the motorcyclist's turn. Many AMA members and everyday commuter
riders cursed the chopper crowd for tarring all motorcyclists under their
greasy, unshaven brush. Hard-working family men who might have ridden a

Choppers Unlimited's finished product is meant to be ridden and ridden hard. Paul Martinez

loud, unmuffled, and barely legal chopper simply because they thought the machine looked cool found themselves subject to roadside inspections and harassment from the neighbors.

But in this outsider status, some chopper riders reveled. Sure, "The Man" might have taken too much notice of your machine, but hey, that's what it's all about, showing class and freaking out the squares, man. "All week long, you had your boss or your family or your wife or some damn body telling you what to do. Things were different then; guys didn't wear long hair and cutoffs. You toed the line or you didn't get any work. When we got a chance to get out on our sickles on the weekends, well, we just let loose. We had a lot of steam to blow off, and boy, did we ever," founding Boozefighters member John "J.D." Cameron told an interviewer in 1979, and his words still ring true with custom

motorcycle riders today. You may spend the week in a necktie or coveralls or staring dead-eyed into a computer monitor. But on weekends, the chopper still provides a sense of escape that cars, boats, or Rollerblading just can't match.

It was the same desire to transcend the travails of the workweek through close identification with a highly personalized vehicle that fueled Latino lowrider culture, the 300-watt boom trucks of the inner city, and the scooters and race-replica street bikes of British mods and rockers in the 1960s. This need to be noticed and recognized at play had, since the earliest days of motor sports, caused otherwise respectable young men to abandon propriety and social convention at the swing of a kick starter.

"They would ride in city or open country with their mufflers cut out, or in numerous cases absolutely devoid of muffling attachment. In some instances, it was the rider's desire for noise, or to bring attention to the fact that he owned a motorcycle; in other instances it was the owner's desire for more power; but whichever case, this offense in principle and in conjunction with that of unsuitable attire has done more to retard the advancement of motorcycling in general than all other arguments combined," wrote *Harper's* magazine correspondent Alfred H. Hatsch. Hatsch, by the way, wrote those words after spending a weekend with a group of motorcycle riders in 1909. The more things change. . . .

Over the next decade, this disparate blend of cultural, political, and social influences—and a little help from a burgeoning youth market—was about to take choppers on a wild ride from the fringe elements of motorcycling straight to the fringed jackets and mod fashions of the psychedelic era. During the 1960s and '70s, widespread acceptance of choppers would forever change the look and style of motorcycling in America and, later, the rest of the world. But notoriety, in time, nearly killed the chopper.

Choppers Unlimited hasn't strayed far from the custom chopper movement's roots; its motorcycles are still designed for the working man who can't afford the latest billet accessories and big-name concept bikes.

Paul Martinez

Chapter 2

Truckin' through the '60s

Choppers Rule

Previous pages

A flamed, rigid custom from Big Mike Rouse's BMC Choppers. Rouse, who likes to pull wheelies on his bikes, prefers that his machines perform as well as they look.

Quinn Shields/BMC

Chrome polished, bedroll packed, it's time for a ride. Packs of choppers were becoming a common sight in California in the 1960s.

Dain Gingerelli

from Europe, Japan, and Australia are common at Denver's, where modern, updated versions of their classic choppers are now on sale, replete with drilled disc brakes, adjustable handlebars, and the signature "mile-long" springer forks. "Guys were going crazy for our stuff. We made them anywhere from about 8 to 10 inches longer than stock because they were all steel and they got to be pretty heavy front ends. The guys all wanted narrow, 21-inch front wheels, jockey shifts, and tall ape-hanger handlebars in chrome dog-bones risers. Then we'd Frisco (or remount a Sportster gas tank for a higher profile) and put on a chrome sissy rail on the back. All of that stuff we had to make by hand," Porras said. Producing these one-off parts was time con-suming and costly, but it didn't stop hundreds of choppers being built this way all across Southern California.

Though many latter-day chopper enthusiasts have adopted a Harleys-only approach to building customs, Porras and other early builders attest to see-ing all sorts of motorcycles, from Indians to Ariels and even the odd BSA or Honda CB 450 being put to the torches in the early days. In fact, Denver's received so many requests for custom rigid frames and front ends for foreign-made motorcycles that Mullins had little choice but to launch an assembly line chopper frames business in 1967. In a couple of years, Denver's was of-fering rigid frames with raked and stretched headstocks for 15 different mo-torcycles, and soon thereafter, chromed springer forks that were much lighter than the unwieldy, vulcanized Ford/H-D models of a few years before.

Just as small, hot-rod auto body shops had specialized in removing the chrome trim and streamlining the bodywork that Detroit's finest had built into cars, chopper shops like Denver's set out to redesign the motorcycle chassis in their own vision. When working on a factory frame, unsightly mounting tabs were removed for a cleaner appearance. The rough assembly-line welds were smoothed over with layer after layer of body putty, also called "molding." Eventually, molding chopper frames became an art unto itself, with custom builders sometimes enveloping entire gas tanks and fenders in the stuff in an endless—and sometimes bizarre—search for smooth, flowing lines. Where bobbers had been content to simply hacksaw a few inches off of a skirted, full-coverage stock fender, chopper builders added voluptuous "bobtails" or elaborate hexagonal designs.

As is the case today, most 1960s chopper riders weren't content to stop changing their motorcycle at just the cosmetic level. With the chopper's roots firmly placed in the drag-racing world, enhanced performance was as important as obtaining a cool, individualistic profile. When Denver's was besieged with requests to bore and stroke stock 74-cubic-inch Harley-Davidson motors, it soon offered improvised stroker kits to the faithful.

With their signature mile-long springer front ends, Denver Mullins' Denver's Choppers took full advantage of Nevada's long, straight roads. The firm has championed the outlaw longbike look even while others abandoned it as impractical.

Denver's Choppers

Rake set out around 48 degrees and the springer forks kicked out a whopping 30 inches longer than stock, Denver's Mondo Porras says engineering the proper rake and trail dimensions makes for a steady, safe ride.

Denver's Choppers

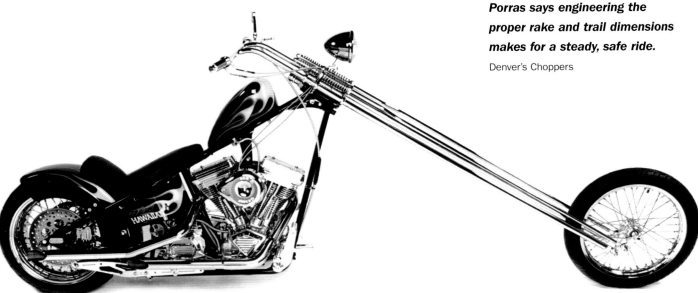

One typical change involved borrowing a set of heavier flywheels from a Harley-Davidson 80-inch ULH Flathead model and installing them in a Panhead or early Shovelhead case. This operation required extensive internal crankcase modifications but allowed the motor to be bored out to 80 inches or more. With some chopper motors previously serving duty as police motorcycles or high-mileage touring mounts, these overly stressed engines sometimes balked at having their cylinder walls further stressed by extensive reboring. Twisting a throttle flat-out or challenging a buddy to a drag race could result in a fairly spectacular engine blowup. Shattered cases or holed cylinder walls were not uncommon.

Still, experimenting with performance upgrades quickly became as integral a part of chopper building as a wild paint job and chrome detailing. At Denver's, Porras and Mullins replaced battery-power with tiny, aircraft-style magneto ignitions. Working from a gearshift connected to a motorcycle's generator, the magnetos barely sparked enough electrical power to keep the headlights running (bulbs would grow dim at stoplights and shine brightly again when the throttle was revved!); nevertheless, chopper builders adopted them for their light weight and simplicity. Solid lifters replaced hydraulic ones. And with no aftermarket cams sitting on the local Harley shop's shelves, chopper builders ground custom cams for customers or adapted the racier FLH cams into a vintage Panhead or Knucklehead motor. Though the legendary interchangeability of Harley-Davidson components helped many a chopper project, the lack of aftermarket parts pushed small chopper shops to learn everything from lathe to milling machine operations.

As stroker motors grew to outsized proportions, mechanics made do by installing 1/4-inch aluminum "stroker plates" at the cylinders' base to allow for the lengthy piston strokes required by these big-inch motors. They also stretched the front frame downtubes of chopper frames to allow more room for stroker mills, which, in turn, changed the way choppers looked and handled. With engine heads ported and smoothed for increased combustion, and often sporting homemade organ or shotgun exhaust pipes (without mufflers, of course) these motors were notoriously finicky. In this veritable "laboratory" atmosphere, choppers became test beds for exotic carburetion methods too. Dome-style British S.U. carburetors, popular on Jaguar's XKE sports car, were frequently forced into motorcycle duty, while others fabricated dual manifolds to use twin carburetors.

For its projects, Denver's favored fitting a set of Lake Injectors, an odd piece of equipment resembling a billfold with a chrome velocity stack jutting out of one side. Porras remembers the injectors were tough to start, and a chopper rider who missed the compression stroke while trying to kick-start a

The laid-back riding posture of a chopper necessitated the invention of the King and Queen seat: Elaborate upholstery stitching was a must. Dain Gingerelli

surly, big-inch injected motor would find himself facing a long, sometimes embarrassing wait until the flooded motor sorted itself out.

Naturally, with so much time, money, and self-sacrifice involved in building and riding a chopper, a hierarchy of sorts emerged within the chopper community. Porras said there were few "weekend chopper riders" on the roads in the mid-1960s, because middle-class folks didn't want to be associated with the outlaw images indelibly stamped on choppers. Riding a chopper into a small town where a group of hairy, foul-mouthed Satan's Slaves had made an un-wanted appearance on their choppers a few weeks before could be an unsettling experience for the unsuspecting biker.

Mainstream motorcyclists felt that choppers were, to be frank, an abomination against engineering and common sense. Your average frat brother on his Honda Dream or a middle-aged member of the all-female Motor Maids on an FLH couldn't fathom why anyone would willfully disconnect their front brakes or intentionally make their motorcycle louder and flashier. This chasm of style and purpose, how-ever, was a badge of pride to many chopper riders who, in turn, basked in their outsider status. But as the outlaw bik-er gangs, who most often rode choppers, made headlines for various rapes, brawls, and drug offenses, many chopper riders often found themselves denied entry to bars and

Chopper passengers needed to be careful riding so close to the organ exhaust pipes. Ear plugs might not have hurt either. Dain Gingerelli

Handlebars were a source of constant invention for chopper builders. Here, a set of extreme pull-backs made for a La-Z-Boy riding style.
Dain Gingerelli

Like Harley-Davidson's torquey Sportsters, British twins were re-designed as choppers.

Dain Gingerelli

restaurants; and the guy who rode a "chop" because it expressed his individuality might find himself getting more familiar with the local police than he'd ever imagined.

"All the other chopper riders knew that a guy had to pretty much build their own chopper, so there was like a right to keep it on the road," Porras said. "Chopper riders were a pretty elite group back in those days, so sometimes the outlaw clubs would just walk up and take a guy's bike if they didn't feel like he deserved it. They were that serious." With vehicle modification laws seldom endorsing tall handlebars, unmuffled exhausts, and sky-high sissy bars, chopper riders could count on being subject to roadside police inspections. The constant hassles of riding a chopper, plus the fear and loathing—to borrow a phrase from *Hell's Angels* author Hunter S. Thompson—that everyday "citizens" held for chopper riders further distanced the custom bike crowd from the masses.

But if the outlaws thought they could keep the chopper aesthetic to themselves, they were in for a rude awakening; they hadn't envisioned the arrival of a young motorcycling visionary from Los Angeles named Tom Mc-Mullen. A whiz kid in the performance car parts industry, McMullen expanded his company, Automotive Electrical Engineering (AEE), to include replicas of some of the outrageous—and sought-after—chopper parts he'd seen rolling along the streets of Southern California. Though some have credited the motion picture industry with spreading the chopper gospel to regions of the world where the term "chopper" was still a slang term for a set of grandma's dentures, the almost overnight worldwide growth of the style could not have occurred without parts suppliers like Mc-Mullen. Films like *Wild Angels* and *Born Losers* enticed a new generation of would-be outlaws onto two wheels at local drive-ins, but fledgling chopper riders were mostly bereft of the custom parts to turn their otherwise ordinary Triumph Bonnevilles and Harley-Davidson Sportsters into approximations of the bikes they'd seen on screen.

The ever-present tool roll mounted to the triple clamps was a necessity for chopper riders. Wrenching and maintenance were a source of pride for builders. Author's collection

Local fabrication shops such as Denver's Choppers were capable but scarce. More than that, hiring a seasoned car or bike builder to create a one-of-a-kind motorcycle was well out of the price range of the average biker. Those without well-stocked garages or access to machine shops often made do with poor, homemade custom jobs. Chopping on a budget meant utilizing jury-rigged contraptions like "slugged" front ends, which were threaded

Besides providing passenger support, sissy bars were a place to display totems and personal beliefs. This Panhead rider's dollar sign reflected the serious expense of building a chopper. Mike Seate

Inside the workshop at Denver's Choppers. Guiseppi Roncen

"Bondo Mondo" Porras, chopper builder and unofficial historian who has led the custom bike movement for four decades.

Guiseppi Roncen

lead extensions shoved into the front fork's lower legs to add length. Others fashioned spot-welded sissy bars and chopper forks out of everything from lawn furniture to stolen subway and bus grab rails. Though inventive, these homemade chop jobs offered about the same level of support and safety as a $2.99 folding lawn chair.

As legend has it, McMullen was at home one summer in a full-leg cast recuperating from a motorcycle accident when friends inquired where they could buy components similar to those on his hand-built, chopped Harley. Bored, McMullen began welding sissy bars and handlebars for friends until he realized the instant "cha-ching!" potential of stamping out hundreds, if not thousands, of similar parts for the consumer aftermarket. Though it's hard to imagine a scarcity of aftermarket parts in these days of book-length custom parts catalogs and nearly infinite online- and mail-order suppliers, McMullen's idea was truly revolutionary. AEE's launched its motorcycle parts division in 1967 and McMullen quickly set about drafting designs for the AEE line of chopper parts and hired a team of welders and chrome-plating laborers for his new facility on Anaheim's Via Burton Avenue.

He manufactured rigid chopper frames for Harley-Davidson's 74-cubic-inch motors, which sold for around $275 each—no small sum for the average biker to round up in the late '60s. Though these tubular steel frames sold respectably, McMullen was besieged with requests for still cheaper components. A crew of his designers happened upon the more affordable idea of a bolt-on hardtail, a triangular rear frame section that would change even the stodgiest stock machine into a low-riding custom in a matter of hours. Owners simply chopped off the rear swing arm, shock-absorber mounts, and fender rails with a torch or hacksaw and bolted or welded in their place one of AEE's instant hardtail kits. These insta-choppers may have been of questionable structural integrity, and the rigid struts that firms like Jammer Cycle Parts and AEE popularized—chromed steel posts that bolted into a stock motorcycle's shock-absorber mounts—may have caused otherwise decent-handling bikes to carve corners with all the agility of a Safeco shopping cart, but they sold as fast as manufacturers could make them.

Along with the initial flood of orders that arrived in response to AEE ads placed in automotive magazines (motorcycle monthlies still considered choppers taboo), McMullen also received a few orders for parts that he hadn't yet considered, such as replacement steel gas tanks for stock motorcycles. For years, fledgling chopper builders made do with Harley-Davidson's notoriously thirsty Sportster gas tank, a curvaceous 2.25-gallon fuel carrier that lent itself well to many custom applications. Smaller "peanut"-style gas tanks, so named for the resemblance to Georgia's favorite tuber, were another chopper builder's favorite. However, peanut tanks were often cannibalized from small-displacement British off-road machines such as BSA's 441 Victor and were in short supply. AEE's chic hexagonal gas tanks, high- and low-tunnel Sportster tanks (which offered varied mounting profiles for chopper builders) were cheap, well-made, and arrived in the post ready for whatever custom paint a builder could throw their way.

AEE responded to an increasing number of requests for complete chopper motorcycle kits for a wide variety of imported bikes. The tens of thousands of Triumphs, Nortons, and BSAs that had threatened Harley-Davidson's market dominance in the late 1950s and early 1960s were, by now, in the hands of restless, youthful riders who were also catching the chopper bug in record numbers. With comparatively conservative styling and little in the way of aftermarket custom parts available, save the odd pair of taller-than-stock handlebars or roarty exhausts, British bike riders, unlike Harley-Davidson builders, were hamstrung by limited chopping options.

McMullen helped the Brit riders catch up to their Harley-mounted brethren by quickly issuing an entire showroom's worth of British chopper parts. The narrow, twin-cylinder Triumph motors looked handsome in a rigid frame, and when fitted with aftermarket, shorty drag pipes, they issued an exhaust note that was nearly as impressive as that of a much larger bike. Because the reliability of Harley-Davidsons went on a rapid decline after the Milwaukee firm was purchased by bowling equipment manufacturer American Machine Foundry (AMF) in 1969, many chopper builders looked elsewhere for power plants. That same year Honda, which—like Suzuki, Yamaha, and later, Kawasaki—had entered the American market with a series on decidedly un-threatening, small-displacement commuter bikes, shocked the domestic bike scene with its fast, powerful, and reliable CB 750.

Though the Honda's double overhead cam, in-line four-cylinder motor was wide by V-twin standards, in a few years chopper builders were stripping

"I'm sorry, I guess I expected too much when I saw those twelve-inch extenders on your bike."

A little chopper humor. Academics and intellectuals also would ponder the psycho-sexual motivations for extended motorcycle forks.

Easyriders magazine

After WWII, bobber riders displayed German military insignia as a source of postwar pride. By the 1960s, swastikas and Maltese crosses were there to freak out the squares and cops. Guiseppi Roncen

motors from crashed (and the occasional stolen) CB 750s into choppers with increasing regularity. By the time McMullen's business had grown to require a new, larger facility in nearby Placentia, he had almost single-handedly launched the chopper mail-order revolution—a mechanical do-it-yourself craze still unparalleled in motorcycling history.

McMullen can't get full credit for founding this trend, however, because dozens of other parts wizards realized the financial rewards of the assembly-line production of chopper parts during this period. Arlen Ness, then a young, ambitious bike builder living in California's Bay Area, was gaining a reputation for creating head-turning custom Harleys, starting with one motorcycle, his 1947 Harley-Davidson Knucklehead. He admitted in a 1997 interview in *Cycle World* magazine that he'd often visit the hippie coffee shops and nightclubs in and around San Francisco for inspiration. A new, different vanguard of artistic expression was in full effect in California then with its bold colors and organic lines adorning everything from flyers advertising hippie rock bands to elaborately engraved water bongs. Ness incorporated pop-art symbols from peace signs to Peter Max–style psychedelic artwork onto his bike.

"I probably customized that thing five times," Ness said, referring to his old Knucklehead. "Every year, I would take it apart and redo it in a different way or a different fashion because I didn't have the money for another bike." Ness was typical of the early chopper builders in that he seldom let a lack of funds defy his creative impulses. Most were self-taught at welding, which came in handy for fashioning extended forks and sissy bars and for chopping and raking frames, while bodyman's skills, usually picked up while building hot-rod cars, were essential for molding gas tanks and frames for the era's all-important seamless look.

"It was basically a fad back then. A lot of guys came back from the service and wanted to get into choppers after they'd heard about them through the motorcycle grapevine or saw one in a movie somewhere," Ness said.

At first, there were few full-blown, ground-up customs, Ness says. The average rider simply couldn't afford to go gonzo with a limited budget, so many chopper riders sufficed by altering whatever components would be guaranteed to generate the most stares and admiration.

And generating stares was a big part of what the chopper was all about. British chopper enthusiast and outlaw biker Maz Harris often wrote of the thrill of being stared at by pedestrians while rolling slowly down a quiet village road, basking in the stoic, slightly stoned facade of indifference his group affected while riding their choppers. Granted, there exists a certain drama to riding a chopper, a curbside form of performance art that starts the moment a chopper rider turns on the fuel petcocks and tickles his carburetor. He's just swaggered off the bar stool, making sure the broad in the too-tight jeans was watching, before throwing a leg across the narrow, piked saddle.

Five grand worth of chrome, sweat-equity, and knee-deep lacquer is catching the glare of the streetlights, and a few kids might have gathered to watch your chopper rumble to life. The elaborate ritual of starting goes as follows: Push the kick starter through twice to align the compression stroke; twist the key in the ignition; give it a little throttle; and then, Whoomp! a fast thrust on the kicker and the street is bathed in unmuffled sound. Click up the long, almost horizontal kickstand, jerk your head to the side so your ponytail falls over

Except for the high-quality chrome, this bobber could have stepped right out of the 1940s.
Guiseppi Roncen

A '40s-style bobber with a '60s-era engine ridden by a '90s skate punk: pure postmodernism at work.

Guiseppi Roncen

Unbeknownst to U.S. chopper riders, their deigns and attitudes were quickly finding an audience across the Atlantic. This Swedish chopper rider attempts a familiar biker gesture at an early European rally but uses the wrong finger.

Guiseppi Roncen

your shoulders just so, and slowly, deliberately, you roar off down Main Street, leaving a trail of gawking onlookers and high-octane exhaust noise in your wake. It was a scenario that turned everyday mechanics and laborers into instant local heroes. For a generation of motorcyclists, this image proved too much to resist.

In a few years, Arlen Ness, among others, capitalized on the widespread appeal of the chopper by offering mass-produced versions of his fenders and gas tanks to eager chopper builders across the country. Ness' dislike of the form-over-function longbike led to his use of shortened springer front ends. These lent a bike the stripped-down chopper look but did so while maintaining a relatively safe ride. His early frames featured stretched headstocks but somewhat conservative rake designs that came to be known as the "digger"- or "Norcal"-style chopper. Fiberglass rear fenders, tiny flat-bottom Sportster gas tanks, and fanciful paint schemes, often infused with gold-leaf detailing, rounded out the "Ness look." Today, Ness has taken these same sophisticated designs to places where few early chopper builders would have imagined possible: His motorcycles have been featured in art museums and technology journals, while Arlen Ness Enterprises is perhaps the best-known custom parts name in the industry.

At roughly the same time that Ness was building his international chopper empire and McMullen was making chopper parts as available as Hula-Hoops and Ronco's Dial-O-Matic, Forking by Frank, located in Evanston, Illinois, was making extended fork tubes available for chopper riders. These well-made stock replacements helped many a budget-conscious chopper builder achieve the laid-back profile they'd been searching for. Add a tiny white leather seat for a little flash, find a backstreet body shop to render a five-color paint job and some shorty fenders, and that well-used FLH Police Special was well on its way to becoming a counterculture icon.

When Frank Stankovich, a small, Midwestern bicycle parts shop operator, decided to manufacture well-made, extended replacement tubes for motorcycle forks in 1966, there was no competition, says his wife, Mary. After hearing many complaints about the lack of quality fork tubes and witnessing the results of crashes caused by inferior custom parts, Frank decided to make the switch from bicycles to motorcycles. His timing couldn't have been better. Riders, many of them "just wanting to be different, or wanting to look like the outlaw guys they saw in those biker movies," lined up for miles, most of them for forks 6, 8, and often 12 inches longer than stock, said Mary, who still runs the world-renowned shop.

From the beginning, Frank's knew its parts would be scrutinized by state vehicle inspectors who were responding to the chopper craze with roadside inspections and ever-stricter equipment violations laws. But Frank's tubes, lathe-turned from rolled steel, proved satisfactory in even the most conservative states, Mary said. It was about time too. The market was, at the time, flooded with all sorts of inferior chopper contraptions, many of them offering not much more than unusual

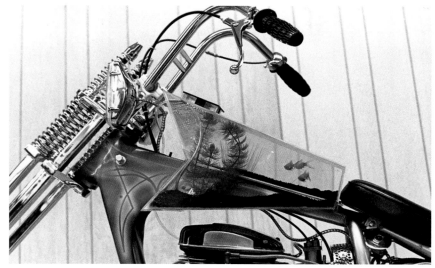

looks in the place of actual usability. Fork extenders, for example, made a brief appearance before being dismissed as too dangerous. These simple, rigid struts bolted into a set of stock triple clamps with no damping whatsoever made for a ride similar in intensity to a Waring blender set on "chop."

It may have looked cool to remove a front brake and run a tiny 3-inch spool for a radically clean front end, but Frank's extended tubes allowed riders to adopt a chopper profile while still utilizing the stock front brakes (required by law in California as of 1971 but frequently circumvented by registering a chopper through a friend's address in Nevada or Arizona). Though Frank was killed in a plane crash in 1976 during his company's peak years, Mary is grateful that choppers have recently come back into vogue for a new generation of riders. "We're still the only people making fork tubes for the Harley FXWG and FXE up to 12 inches longer than stock. In the last four years, I've almost been unable to keep up with the demand," she said.

Inspiration from inside the fish tank—this chopper builder painted his gas tank to match his aquarium. Dain Gingerelli

Hand-bent, two-into-four organ pipes, fringed leathers, and a smile: Swedish choppers circa 1969. The BSA and Royal Enfield (second from left) proved that any bike could—and would—be chopped. Guiseppi Roncen

Stankovich and others realized that parts manufacturers finally had the upper hand in the chopper game. Instead of riders searching endlessly for the right parts to build their dream machines, there was a glut of parts suppliers searching for customers. For a while, supply and demand rode along happily, side by side with the demand for choppers and custom parts soon revolutionizing motorcycling, both on the street and from the major manufacturers. But in time, the widespread exposure of the chopper would nearly sound its death knell.

How Long Is Too Long?
Extended Forks Stretch Out

Extended rake helped choppers ride better on the highways, but you wouldn't want to make a fast U-turn on a tight road.

Dain Gingerelli

Since the emergence of the stretch chopper in the 1960s, psychologists have attempted to link motorcycles with extended front forks to some sort of deeply repressed psychosexual inadequacies. And though this may be mere speculation, the headshrinkers do raise an interesting question about choppers: How long is too long when it comes to front forks?

According to Phoenix, Arizona's, Paul Yaffee, one of the country's leading chopper builders, motorcycle forks can be safely kicked out 12 inches or more, allowing, of course, that the frame has been raked and stretched accordingly.

"The difference between old school choppers and the incredible machines being built today is all in understanding the geometry of how a long bike works," Yaffee explained with all the authority of a college professor. "It used to be, guys would just slap a long fork on a chopper and wonder why it didn't handle. What you have to do is put some science to it. If you really study the geometry, you can run a fork 10- or 20-inches-over stock that handles as safely and smoothly as a stock motorcycle if you get the right three or four inches of trail."

Many of Yaffee's stretch choppers utilize rigid frames in the classic chopper tradition, and whether they're ridden at highway speeds or spend their lives trundling through saloon parking lots, he swears their stability remains constant due to carefully designed frames. Stretch, when added to a motorcycle's front downtubes, raises the front fork mounting points and offsets the extreme length of a long front end. Rake, or the angle of the headstock in relation to the front axle, must be lengthened to offset the length of longer front forks.

A lack of planning when it came to rake and trail dimensions was what made many early choppers feel so front-end heavy at low speeds, Yaffee said. Raking and stretching frames is no simple task: Factory engineers spend thousands of man-hours designing motorcycle chassis for sharp, precise handling. Achieving a working compromise between chopper looks and roadworthy practicality often takes years of chassis design, complex knowledge of frame dynamics, and a talented welder.

One answer to the front-end flop dilemma was reached by Sweden's most famous chopper technician, Torben "Tolle" Dehnisch, who, in the 1980s, perfected raked triple trees that allowed chopper builders to adjust their frame's geometry according to fork length. Tolle and other Scandinavian builders favored some of the longest front forks ever designed for a working motorcycle, commonly reaching 20 and 30 inches longer than stock and utilizing 45- and even a near-horizontal 54-degree rakes. An additional 8 degrees of rake in the fork triple clamps added stability and reduced low-speed flop. These eight-foot long mega-choppers came to characterize the so-called Swedish chopper look and were only possible in a country where vehicle inspection laws were virtually nonexistent.

Mondo Porras of Denver's Choppers in Henderson, Nevada, laughs at the term "Swedish choppers" because Denver's was the first to build bikes with 20- and 30-inch-over forks back in the 1970s. Still in business over 30 year later, Denver's chops are easily recognizable for their sleek lines and raked-out profiles. A typical Denver's rigid frame bike runs a 3.5-inch stretch in the front frame downtubes—originally created, Porras said, to help high-mounted or "Friscoed" gas tanks clear the handlebars—and as much as 43 degrees of rake in the neck. That makes for a very relaxed, slow-steering motorcycle at low speeds, but out on the two-lane blacktop where choppers were meant to roll, the riding position is sure, stable, and as comfortable as a well-worn easy chair.

"It takes years, even decades, for a chopper builder to understand rake and trail, and only from getting it wrong a few times can they start getting it right," said Porras, who uses a system of computer-aided jigs to weld his hardtail chopper frames. Today, Denver's makes their frame tubing from a chrome-moly steel that yields little to road variances or power-train stresses. The frames are a study in minimalist strength. As a result, Porras claims that even Denver's longest stretch choppers are built to such exacting dimensions that they can turn tight circles even in a confined space. "You've got to experiment with rake and stretch, but there's a sweet spot you can find that will make the

"There's really no limit to how long a front end can be as long as it's done right," says Denver's Choppers' Mondo Porras.

Paul Martinez

bike handle real smooth. I built a bike for a guy in Hawaii that was like, 54-inches-over stock, and he can ride it anywhere."

Rake and trail dimensions are imperative for proper handling for the long bike, agrees Mike Rouse of Big Mike's Choppers, who was the first of the current crop of custom bike builders to relaunch the mail-order chopper. He is relatively conservative when it comes to adding length to his laid-back motorcycles. "We try and stick to extended front ends at around six or maybe eight inches. When they get much longer than that, you have to rake them out more than 40 degrees, and that creates too much front end flop," Rouse said. With many BMC customers on the mature side, he tends to err on the side of control and caution rather then forsaking low-speed rideability in favor of radical, mile-long front-end looks.

"If you have a 20-over front end and a guy is riding out on the highway and takes his hands off the bars, there's a good chance all of that front-end weight will flop on him and he's going down," Rouse said. Several other top chopper builders have also eschewed the radically long front end look, including Arlen Ness, who claims to "have never really gone for that whole long bike look," and Jesse James, who builds his post-modern choppers to ride fast and corner somewhat sharper than the choppers and custom bikes rolling through his native Long Beach a generation before. Not that James is beyond stretching out a bike when the mood hits him: His personal ride for several years was a purple, hardtail stretch chopper with 12-inch-over-stock Wide Glide forks, jockey shift, and a rake of almost 40 degrees. A six-inch stretch in the neck made

for a very Peter Fonda profile and a bike that actually bounced over bumps as the forks were almost too long to utilize their damping. "Once you start getting into those really long forks, it takes a lot of strength to ride the bike properly. Most people don't want that much hassle while they're riding, so we keep the forks short and controllable," James says. Short forks or long, it's all really a question of what suits your riding style.

Chapter 3

Too Hip to Be Cool

Choppers Nearly Die of Overexposure

A custom conundrum. This chopped 1973 Harley-Davidson Sportster looks great, but the stock frame rake is a less-than-perfect match for the 12-inch-over-stock springer front end. Such designs meant that steering could be heavy and clumsy at low speeds.

Dain Gingerelli

Previous pages
Hundreds of hours of bodywork and sheet-metal fabrication went into this supercharged Triumph Bonneville chop. How the one-of-a-kind monopod handlebars affected steering is anybody's guess. Dig the built-in 8-track tape deck!

Dain Gingerelli

By the early 1970s, there were literally dozens of entrepreneurs answering the call for well-crafted, standardized custom chopper parts. Aftermarket houses like California's Paughco, D&D Distributors, and seat-maker Gary Bang competed for a growing custom-cycle dollar with big-money concerns like Minnesota's Drag Specialties. These second-generation chopper parts were mostly of a higher quality than the earlier offerings from AEE, Vista Chopper Products, and other early aftermarket houses. Drag Specialties CEO Tom Rudd, for instance, was a successful motorcycle drag racer who was among the first aftermarket houses to establish a rapport with the engineering departments of the major manufacturers. By starting from a small, Minneapolis-based shop in 1968, Rudd had developed relatively deep pockets by the mid-1970s and had an R&D department full of recent-model motorcycles to use as development mules for custom and chopper accessories. As a result, Drag Specialties parts tended to fit stock machines well and last for much longer than comparable parts from many competitors.

Drag Specialties' popular king and queen seats for Harleys had their legendary tufted stitching made from real cowhide, not vinyl, and seat pans that fit snugly against Harley-Davidson's frames. Its exhaust pipes were made not just for show or maximum noise but also to meet increasingly strict emission statutes and complement the overall character and flow of a custom bike. Rudd had, by the late 1970s, developed a multi-million-dollar aftermarket empire, just 15 years after patenting designs on Maltese-cross taillights, dual rectangular headlights, and other accouterments of the chopper era.

Gone were the parts with mounting-flange holes that didn't line up as advertised and those late-night tantrums over kick-start levers that gouged custom-painted frames every time a chopper was started. Real draftsmen were now increasingly in charge of setting up elaborate jigs to make springer and girder front ends that were quite an improvement over the stock rigid forks with extensions welded into the rails.

One Californian firm, first known as D&D Distributing and later as Jammer Cycle Parts (see *Easyriders* sidebar), billed itself as a place with "everything you need to know about designing a chopper." Their 150-page catalogs, full of glossy color glamour shots of girls on custom choppers, could back up that claim easily. In addition to offering their customers thousands of parts, from chromed oil tanks to ornate brass fuel petcocks that resembled plumbing fixtures from a Victorian powder room, the annual *Jammer's Handbook* contained useful articles on constructing choppers—using its own selection of accessories, of course. A creation of California's Paisano Publications, the *Jammer's Handbook* offered parts for imported as well as domestic

Chopped, raked, stretched, and molded, the 1970s heralded in an era of unlimited chopper customizing. It would not last forever. Dain Gingerelli

Whoa, there! This Honda CB 450 chopper was the result of a burgeoning aftermarket that provided parts to chop just about any motorcycle. Crosswinds were to be avoided!

Dain Gingerelli

choppers, unlike *Easyriders,* which adopted an intolerant party line toward choppers of non-American origin. Business being business, Jammer was in it to sell chopper parts and did so by the trainload. With stories advising chopper builders on "How to Tell the Difference between Harley Engines" and "Secrets of Buying a Safe Springer," Mil Blair's *Jammer's* combined the nuts and bolts instruction of custom motorcycle building with the irreverent, sometimes druggy, lifestyle journalism that would later come to characterize numerous custom chopper magazines. Blair, now semiretired, recalls how launching *Easyriders* magazine was almost an accident resulting from the success of his *Jammer's* catalogs. Along with two chopper-building buddies, Joe Teresi and Lou "Spider" Kimzey, Blair experimented with adding the odd seminude cheesecake shot and bawdy cartoon to the *Jammer's Handbook*, offering almost instructional lifestyle advice to go with a customer's new chopper.

"We put together some articles and had a guy write some "biker fiction," and the next thing you know, we had *Easyriders* magazine. That turned out to be a better seller than our [*Jammer's*] catalogs," Blair said with a laugh.

Despite the relatively low-effort process advertised in these early chopper parts catalogs, turning a stock motorcycle into a chopper was still an expensive, time-consuming project. In the 1973 *Jammer's Handbook*, rigid frames were advertised for just $275—a price that, by today's standards, sounds almost surreally cheap. But considering that good-condition, second-hand Harleys could be picked up for as little as $600, it seems amazing that so many thousands of motorcycles were given the full custom treatment.

It must also be noted that, while chopper lifestyle magazines of the day attempted to portray a racially homogenous view of motorcycle customizing—portraying the chopper as the whitest thing this side of a tractor pull contest—Southern California's vibrant ethnic communities lent their own twists to the chopper craze. Mexican and Mexican-American car customizing shops had long been at the forefront of the hot-rod culture, turning out elaborate, almost baroque lowriders as early as the 1940s. They had been primarily responsible for making the customized car a mark of social rebellion. The step to customizing motorcycles was, by the 1960s, a small one indeed. Denver's Mondo Porras attests to choppers being popular in Mexico,

Altering frame geometry was expensive and time-consuming. This Canadian Shovelhead owner made do with a rigid, 10-inch-over front end and ape-hanger handlebars. Mike Seate

helped along by that country's notoriously relaxed motor code enforcement. The ornate bolts and nuts and intricately upholstered seats, the elaborate gas tank murals and the richly contoured molding on chopper frames can all be traced, in varying degrees, to Southern California's Latino custom scene.

African-American chopper builders also were busy during the 1970s, with Howard "Tree" Slayton and South Central Los Angeles' Sugar Bear among the most prominent longbike custom builders. A big proponent of mounting undersized front wheels to his hand-welded springer forks, Sugar

Bear was among the first to adopt this style to choppers—a look adopted from the inner-city lowrider practice of mounting the smallest wheels possible on a custom car in order to better display chromed wheel wells and detail work. On the whole, all of these disparate influences contributed to the classic chopper look.

In addition to the various ethnic influences on choppers, McMullen, Rudd, Ness, and dozens of others were helped along by a seismic shift in the nation's youth culture during this period. The Baby Boom generation, which had been raised on a steady diet of network TV and middle-class comfort and conformity, were questioning the sacred cows of their parents' generation, and, naturally, Southern California had been the flash point for a new political and social consciousness.

The "youthquake" that spawned psychedelic musicians like Jimi Hendrix and The Doors, that gave birth to the experimental drug culture and the sexual revolution, also handily rejected the family sedans and comfortable touring bikes favored by the squares. In their endless search for a new identity, youth took to the chopper. And unlike the hard-core outlaw gang members and chopper builders who originated the look, the new generation chopper riders were likely to have plenty of money to spend on their new hobby.

In recent years, many old-school chopper enthusiasts have lamented the "appropriation" of their blue-collar hobby by upper-class interlopers—Rich Urban Bikes, or RUBs as they're called today—but this is nothing new.

Thousands of chromed, five-spoke Invader mag wheels were sold during the chopper's heyday. Few have survived rust and road miles. Mike Seate

Many of the counterculture revolutionaries who comprised the hippie generation and lived in San Francisco's Haight-Ashbury district were upper middle-class kids from indistinguishable suburbs, looking for higher highs and lower lows as campus revolutionaries and street culture denizens. Quite a few found solace and identity in the chopper movement, especially after the 1969 release of the low-budget chopper travelogue *Easy Rider.* Starring Dennis Hopper and Peter Fonda as two wayfaring hippie drug dealers in search of the elusive (and deadly) "real America," *Easy Rider* was the cinematic equivalent of Jack Kerouac's *On the Road,* living proof that one could shake off the constraints of workaday society and redefine one's self through wanderlust.

Choppers had been the staple of biker movies from the days of Roger Corman's *Wild Angels* in 1966, but *Easy Rider* forever cemented an image of long, stretched-out motorcycles—and their equally laid-back riders—into the public's imagination. Though Fonda's Harley-Davidson Panhead, dubbed "Captain America," and Hopper's orange-and-flame Panhead lowrider are probably moviedom's best-known motorcycles, both of the machines used in the film were stolen just days before the film's release. Neither machine was ever recovered. Ironically, and fitting for a pair of well-known California choppers, the bikes were reportedly dismantled and sold for parts. That a biker or two might

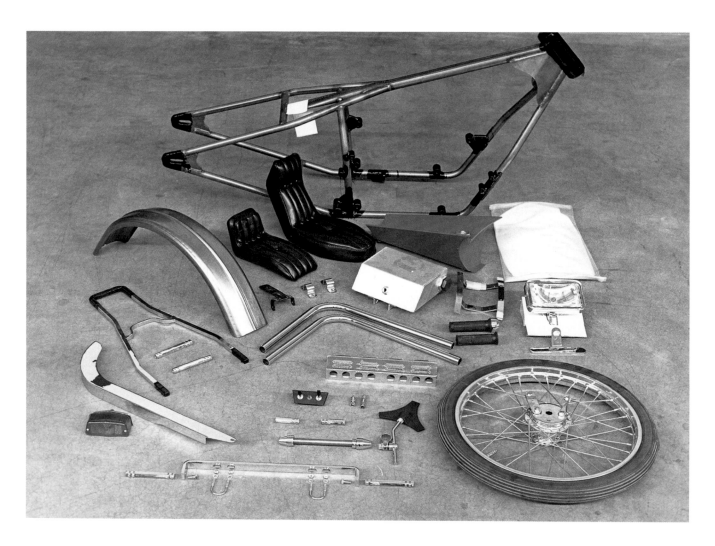

As the demand for chopper parts exploded, clever entrepreneurs like Placentia, California's, Tom McMullen answered back in the 1970s with do-it-yourself chopper kits. Only $475, postage paid!

Dain Gingerelli

well have watched *Easy Rider* at a drive-in on a motorcycle made from parts of those very bikes is testament to the fluidity of the custom bike scene.

Nevertheless, *Easy Rider*'s message of self-exploration and freedom found through riding a handcrafted chopper caught on with a larger segment of the general public than the filmmakers ever could have anticipated. Produced for a measly $340,000, the film has, to date, grossed more than $55 million. And the filmmakers weren't the only people getting rich from the country's obsession with all things long, low, and chromed. By 1974 Tom McMullen was being feted by local chambers of commerce throughout Southern California and had taken to traveling by private helicopter he even appeared in his own house publications attired in "handmade Edwardian business suits."

In many ways, *Easy Rider* was strikingly similar to the music videos offered by MTV, VH-1, and other pop culture outlets of today: It was clearly selling young Americans an image, lifestyle, and soundtrack, lacking only the prerequisite marketing tie-ins we'd expect today. Slow moving and practically plotless, the film reads like a two-hour advertisement for marijuana, verbal non sequiturs, and chopper riding across sun-drenched landscapes.

Riders with no patience for chrome and polish created the rat chopper. Check out the FLH rear fender mounted backwards to the springer forks and cool ammo box saddlebags!

Mike Seate

Which is all that thousands of young men and women who had never before even considered riding a motorcycle—let alone something as alien and unconventional as a chopper—needed to see. That their parents and an older generation of motorcyclists still looked down their noses at these overwrought, stripped-down motorcycles only made choppers more attractive to rebellious youngsters. Though it didn't happen overnight, in a few months time, chopped versions of everyday commuter bikes were springing up on college campuses and

One of AEE's Honda 750 chopper-in-a-box kits still up and running 30 years later. Few have survived the years in such fine condition.

Kim Love

The author's first chopper, a 1969 XLCH with magneto ignition, circa 1980, featured Invader mags and 8-inch-over forks by Franks. Ill-fitting jeans were an aftermarket accessory.

Mike Seate

parked dramatically in front of neighborhood bars and coffee shops from Los Angeles to London.

Motorcyclists who might have entered the sport due to Honda's congenial "You Meet the Nicest People . . . " campaign were now fitting extended fork tubes to their Honda CB 350s. At Sears department stores, customers could purchase cheap knockoffs of Peter Fonda's stars-and-stripes Captain America helmet and kids from coast to coast were imitating Dennis Hopper by wearing more fringed leather than Buffalo Bill's Wild West Show.

Suddenly, choppers were becoming fashionable with middle-class kids and a few middle-aged men, which must have confused and mortified the mechanics and custom bike buffs who'd only experienced rebellion before as expressed in chrome and steel. Chopper chic soon reached the media in full swing, with the NFL's hottest star, New York Jets quarterback "Broadway" Joe Namath saddling up for a turn in *C.C. and Company,* a campy little chopper epic filmed in 1972. Film stars from France's Bridgett Bardot to Ann Margaret either posed on or rode their own choppers around town, while rock stars quickly co-opted the rebellion by posing astride a chopper on album covers and promotional posters. Corporate America, always slow to latch on to trends, soon revealed that it too had been studying the chopper for any "cool" that could be derived form the style. Schwinn, the country's oldest bicycle manufacturer, wasted little time offering up "Stingray" bicycles, their gently kicked-out forks and "banana" seats mimicking the chopper forks and king and queen seats of customized street motorcycles. Actor Rob Reiner appeared as "Snake," a lovable but gruff chopper rider in an episode of TV's *Partridge Family,* Revell, a maker of scale-model kits, soon added chopper trikes and motorcycles on toy store shelves alongside their Panzer tanks and Fokker biplanes.

Marx, one of the world's most successful toy manufacturers, chimed in with the Big Wheel children's tricycle. This noisy, rugged little plastic trike was a carefully scaled-down version of the radical three-wheeled choppers that had long been fashioned out of Harley-Davidson's Servi-Car 45-cubic-inch delivery bikes. The Big Wheel's yellow plastic handlebars mimicked the exaggerated rise of classic chopper ape-hangers, and the oversized real wheels featured mock mag wheel graphics.

The British motorcycle industry, by now, was suffering its own problems, having been outdistanced in affordability and performance by the big four

Japanese bikemakers. In a desperate attempt to cash in on the chopper craze, Norton Motors offered a slapdash custom, the "Hi Rider," advertised in magazines with the prerequisite youth-oriented copy and a leggy model in a miniskirt. The poor-selling Hi Rider was, in reality, nothing more than a stock Norton Commando sporting a very incongruous pair of apehanger handlebars—a modification Norton owners had been making themselves for over 25 years.

Longtime chopper builders like Mondo Porras at Denver's Choppers recalls being "too busy to notice" the stretch bike aesthetic making inroads into mainstream culture, but there was a noticeable change in the sorts of customers patronizing Denver's. "All of a sudden you'd see these yuppie guys who'd never turned a wrench in their lives riding choppers. You just knew that somebody else had built those bikes for them, and that made a lot of the original chopper riders pretty mad," he said.

In a move that shocked—and inspired—motorcycle manufacturers around the world, Harley-Davidson introduced its Super Glide model in 1971, a motorcycle directly inspired by the works of backstreet chopper mechanics. The oddly proportioned motorcycle was designed by Willie G. Davidson and rolled into showrooms with a mod red, white, and blue paint job and a torpedo-shaped "Night Train" rear fender that resembled the tail-fins from

Author's Triumph Bonneville chopper with 12-inch-over springer and Amen "Saviour" softail frame. The plunger suspension provided some travel but was terrifying in corners.
Kim Love

Stylin' and profilin' on a Honda CB 750 chopper. The four-cylinder Japanese superbike engine sat wide in a rigid frame, but few riders complained about its powerband or day-to-day reliability. Note organ pipes and mod footwear! Dain Gingerelli

The day of the super-long front end, high sissy bar and stacks is over—most people are finding out that bikes like that may be striking as all hell, but they're a bear to ride.

What's Next For Choppers?

What happens when there's nothing left to chrome except the traffic tickets?

a 1957 Chevy Bel-Air. While chopper riders laughed at the Super Glide's clearly unhip styling, few could deny the factory's inspiration for mating a narrow, aluminum Sportster front end to an FLH frame. It was a move chopper builders had happened upon decades earlier, and many resented the factory for appropriating design elements from a faction of riders from whom it had vehemently tried to distance itself.

The Super Glide was the first of what became known as "factory customs," and the factory touted it as "something as outrageous as a Yippie and as conservative as an Orange County cop." In the ensuing years, Yamaha, Suzuki, Kawasaki, and Honda would offer their own versions of the factory custom, while Harley-Davidson's success with the "safe chopper" concept would spur dozens of "personalized" bikes available straight from the factory. Harley's expanding line of chrome accessories, Screamin' Eagle performance parts, and custom paint programs are a direct result of clever marketing executives appropriating elements of the chopper craze for profit.

Like rap music, tattooing and body piercing would become in the 1990s, choppers entered the mainstream of American

Once the chopper movement got going full swing, riders competed for the title of King Stretch. This guy's 36-inch-over Wide Glide makes him the clear winner. Easyriders *magazine*

92

pop culture, heralded in by the very forces that had derided it a few years before. Staid, respectable motorcyclists who might refuse to wave in return at a long-haired, bell-bottomed chopper rider might not have realized the irony in presenting their kids with Mattel's Hot Wheels Chopsickles toys for Christmas. Harley's FXE Super Glide spawned the FXS Low Rider of 1977 and, in 1980, the FXWG Wide Glide, another factory custom with a design centered around an old-school chopper favorite—this time, stripping the fork shrouds from an FLH front end and chroming the tubes. The Wide Glide even came stock with flame paint, a king and queen seat, and extended fork tubes! And for the first time, Harley-Davidson advertisements were depicting riders who resembled the actual people who had been buying Harleys: A commemorative poster set from 1980 shows riders with beards, bandannas, and denim cutoff vests riding Hogs, a move the factory wouldn't have dreamt of 10 years earlier.

Choppers, it seemed, had finally arrived. Or had they?

There were those who considered the popularity of factory customs and the subsequent growth of the mail-order chopper parts empire the death of "genuine" or "authentic" choppers, of which every component had been painstakingly fabricated by hand. Rebellion isn't really rebellious if everybody's doing it, they reasoned.

Dad may not have felt threatened anymore when a chopper pulled up to take Suzy for a ride in the 1970s, but the chopper's days were nearly over thanks to aggressive anti-chopper legislation. *Easyriders* magazine

Despite the protests of hard-core chopper builders, mainstreaming choppers had resulted in advances in the build quality of custom parts. The Super Glide sold well because a lot of homemade choppers were of questionable design, with builders often choosing a specific rake and trial combination through looks alone. That 12-inch-over front end may look bitchin' with a 40-degree rake and an unknown amount of stretch in the frame, but whether that equation made for a motorcycle that actually rolled down the highway better than it looked was often a system of trial and (a whole lot of) error.

Likewise, a radically extended set of forks without a corresponding frame stretch could cause massive engine lubrication problems with the motors now running less than parallel to the ground. Many chopper builders say that the art of molding frames to hide the seams between gas tanks, fenders, and chassis may have been created for aesthetic purposes, but on more than a few occasions, multiple layers of putty and body filler were used to hide shoddy welds, improperly mounted components, and, occasionally, broken frames.

As the chopper phenomenon spread from the West Coast to places where winter weather created uneven, potholed roads, flimsily constructed chopper forks and frames often buckled when pushed hard. And who can forget the early "softail" frames, popularized by California's Amen Corporation in the 1970s. Unlike Harley-Davidson's own Softail or FXST frames that utilize a pair of horizontally mounted dampers, Amen's odd-looking semi rigid chassis featured a channel at the rear axles that contained a small chrome damping spring. In theory, the Amen Saviour frames offered an improved ride over the unyielding rigid frames, allowing the rear wheel

Chain-link clutch linkage on this suicide-shift Pan/Shovel and an 8-ball gearshifter are pure '60s kitsch. Shovelhead top end hails from 1966 while the cases and four-speed transmission are circa 1948. Butch Lassiter, *IronWorks* magazine

3 inches of vertical travel. But they often resulted in a choppy, unsettling ride with plenty of disconcerting wheel flex in turns.

None of this was lost on the National Highway Traffic Safety Administration and other road-safety organizations at both the federal and state level. Local police forces and traffic safety boards might have been slow to enact legislation to limit motorcycle modifications in the 1960s, but 10 years later, lawmakers increasingly targeted the chopper. Besides laws scrutinizing the height of a motorcycle's handlebars and backrests, cities, including Washington, D.C., enacted a series of tough anti-chopper ordinances in 1971 that all but signaled an end to the "anything goes" period of custom motorcycle building. Other states were quickly enacting mandatory helmet laws for motorcyclists, which put a damper on the plans of many would-be chopper jockeys. Sure, you could ride a chopper wearing a helmet, but where was the fun in that? Some chopper riders attempted to deal with the helmet laws by decorating their headgear with the same ornate metal-flake and flame paint schemes of their motorcycles, while outlaws had for years responded to helmet legislation by mockingly adorning themselves in everything from steel colanders to antique Kaiser helmets, steel spike included. In the Midwest, chopper riders formed fledgling anti-helmet organizations like Citizens Opposed to Oppressive Laws (COOL) and A Brotherhood Against Totalitarian Enactments (ABATE).

Four exhaust pipes and only two cylinders? "Phosphorescence" was bought in 1967 for $295 and customized in period style.

Butch Lassiter, *IronWorks* magazine

Scandinavian bikers on a run, late 1960s. The mix of cafe racers and primitive choppers suggests a scene in flux. Many European chopper riders were exposed to the chopper style only through the movie Easy Rider.
Guiseppi Roncen

What few ex-military Harleys could be rooted out were quickly hunted down and chopped by eager Swedish builders. This original XA springer was extended the hard way—one weld at a time. Guiseppi Roncen

It was a valiant stand against encroachment on a uniquely unfettered subculture, but by the late 1970s, chopper riders from coast to coast could clearly see the writing on the wall.

Discussing a 1973 PBS documentary that attempted to shed light on the country's motorcyclists, *Motorcycle World* magazine noticed, "There were highway riders, city riders and dirt riders and there were two reps from the New York Hell's Angels. Amazingly, all mentioned, at one time or another, that persecuted feeling."

They had good reason to feel persecuted. After two decades of schlock Hollywood cinema that labeled everyone riding a chopper a rapist, drug dealer, or worse, local constabularies weren't taking any chances. Strict vehicle inspection statutes were adopted that specifically addressed chopped

The best part about riding choppers in Europe in the '60s? Nazi helmets were easy to find in second hand stores! Guiseppi Roncen

motorcycles—many riders found that the machines they'd spent two years and several thousand dollars constructing were now deemed illegal in their home states. Their choices were often limited to buying a "factory custom" that was at least fully legal or making some major changes to existing choppers such as adding a front brake and shortening the forks. Or, as many found, they could give up biking entirely.

There were other options. Choppers lost out again and again to the comparatively safer—and less scrutinized—thrills afforded by the growing line of high-performance muscle cars then rolling out of Detroit. Camaros, Chevrolet's SS Chevelle, and the Dodge Super Bee could lay down a strip of rubber outside the local burger joint and provide a place to hang with the ladies, and got you home dry and safe, without being hassled by Officer Friendly.

It didn't help that the letters pages of popular chopper magazines were filled with outraged readers who had landed in jail or in court paying triple-digit fines after simply showing up in the wrong cop's jurisdiction on a chopper. Most chopper riders remember all too well what happened at the end

Postmodern Knucklehead by Canadian chopper builder Tom Langdon of Rumble Customs employs classic springer, mock-Linkert carb on supercharged engine and tiny, almost invisible disc brake. Paul Martinez

of the movie *Easy Rider;* the scenario of being gunned down by a truck full of resentful hillbillies on a lonely stretch of highway was prescient in the minds of many chopper riders for good reason.

"There were very few of us who didn't get some guff from people in cars just for riding a chopper. It got pretty nasty at times. You'd get run into a ditch or people would assume you were in a gang just because your bike had a fancy paint job or a long fork," remembers Dain Gingerelli, a writer and photographer for *Street Chopper* magazine and now the editor of *IronWorks,* a custom Harley and chopper magazine. It was societal schizophrenia at its worst—Dads who'd buy junior a model kit of a California chopper might well try to introduce the local chopper pilot to his front bumper in a fit of anger.

It seemed that the sort of freedom that chopper riders represented was proving too much for America to bear.

In 1980 *Supercycle* magazine, Larry Flynt's own *Easyriders* imitation biker magazine, ran a blistering op-ed piece, "America: Do They Love Us or Hate Us?" pondering among other things whether the lifestyle would eventually be outlawed for good, with the Maximum Cop locking up all the chopper riders and legislating the springer fork out of existence. By the early 1980s, the point was pretty much moot. Once again Harley-Davidson came under attack from a motorcycle market deluged with cheaper, high-performance imports, this time from Japan. Air-cooled American V-Twins just weren't selling to 20 year-olds, who could wrest the biggest cheap thrills from an in-line four cylinder Japanese bike. The chopper press had dwindled or diversified, with McMullen venturing into sporting magazines and auto industry journals. Jammer published its last *Handbook* in the 1980s and many of the outlaw gang members who had provided a backbone for the chopper lifestyle had been jailed. Often entire clubs were dismantled thanks to federal drug laws.

Suddenly, the world changed and left choppers behind.

In the span of a decade, the chopper went from being considered a cool, counterculture icon to a pop-culture leftover, as dated in the early 1980s as platform shoes, bell bottoms, and love beads. There were plenty of choppers still rolling down the highways, but many were converted back into their Fat Bob and stock-length fork versions when a nostalgia craze slowly overtook the custom bike scene. Custom shops found themselves stuck with dusty shelves full of z-bars, organ pipes, and bolt-on hardtails. The future for choppers might have remained a transportation oddity, an artifact from a forgotten past, if not for a small but fanatical foreign market. Somehow, choppers managed to stay alive in Europe and Japan, places where most Americans never imagined they existed.

Flared exhaust collector and stretched oil bag are pure sheet-metal brilliance. Paul Martinez

Myth of the Superbiker
The Emergence of the Chopper Lifestyle Magazines

Artist Dave Mann codified the chopper lifestyle in his romantic biker centerfold paintings in Easyriders magazine. *Easyriders* magazine

As owner and creator of California's AEE Choppers, Tom McMullen knew he had a winning operation going with his mail-order chopper parts business. The only missing link to the young entrepreneur's marketing plan was a means of showcasing his parts and chopper kits to would-be customers halfway across the continent. Mainstream motorcycle magazines were, and are, a conservative lot, and in the politically unsteady waters of the late 1960s, few magazine editors would risk offending the subscribers who favored touring, street, and performance bikes by accepting paid ads from one of those dirty outlaw chopper outfits.

McMullen's idea, though, was not the first time a chopper enthusiast attempted to capitalize on the custom bike craze in print. In 1967 Ed "Big Daddy" Roth, cartoonist, custom car and bike craftsman, and all-around

raconteur, had launched the short-lived but visually stunning *Choppers* magazine. Roth offered readers from coast to coast some of the first detailed technical accounts of chopped motorcycles. For a time he employed legendary hot-rod artist and underground cartoonist Robert Williams as part of the *Choppers* staff, but the magazine never attracted more than a cult following and folded by 1969.

The inventive McMullen had no idea that he was launching a publishing trend that would someday come almost to define motorcycling when he launched *Street Chopper* magazine just as Roth's magazine was folding. *Street Chopper* followed a simple yet brutally effective formula: Each glossy monthly issue drew readers to newsstands with staged photos of bikini-clad young women smiling invitingly at some lean, mean honcho who was riding—predictably—a chopper designed by AEE. For many motorcyclists living far from the streets of Southern California, this was their first static look at chopped motorcycles, bikes they'd previously only seen in biker exploitation films or through the rare newspaper photo.

While ultimately existing as "ad-vertorial," a place for McMullen to showcase his company's products, the magazine soon provided a forum for hundreds of other small-time custom chopper builders and parts fabricators to show their stuff. Ads poured into *Street Chopper,* luring in customers desperate to express their innerselves through "Shorty muffler drag pipes, $49.95 per set, chromed," and "Extended springer front ends, your choice of length, twisted or straight, $199.00."

Street Chopper never produced the sort of circulation figures to threaten the staid readership of more established magazines like *Cycle Guide* or *Motorcyclist*, but the 1969 release of the Peter Fonda/Dennis Hopper road film *Easy Rider* helped further establish the chopper periodicals as a serious force in the magazine industry.

Nearly two years after *Easy Rider* catapulted chopped motorcycles out of the back alleys and into the cultural mainstream, the first issue of *Easyriders* magazine appeared on the newsstands. Billing itself in that premiere issue as "Entertainment for the Swinging Biker," *Easyriders* was the brainchild of Joe Teresi, Lou Kimzey, and Mil Blair, a trio of custom motorcycle fanatics who had been marketing their own line of custom parts through their self-published *Jammer's Handbook*. The Jammer line of chopper parts—initially launched under the D&D Distributors banner—was easily as extensive as McMullen's, and each of the densely illustrated bimonthlies featured seminude female models draped across a series of Jammer choppers. "The guys from Jammer realized that they could add a few articles and some fiction to that format and that's where *Easyriders* magazine came from," said Dave Nichols, current *Easyriders* editor.

The Jammer crew was well aware of the growth potential in creating a "lifestyle" publication for the wild, unconventional types who founded the chopper craze.

With their own ideas about sex and drugs (the more the better of both, please), distinct styles of dress, behavior, and music, the chopper riders were a ripe audience to cater to, ready for a magazine of their own. The inaugural issue of *Easyriders* describes a contributing editor's job as "reporting on the fun side of owning a chopper—be it a beer run with one percenters, or explaining the chopper's phallic appeal to women." Besides providing valuable how-to information on building choppers and full-color feature articles about cutting-edge custom motorcycles and the men who built them, many readers were drawn to *Easyriders* for the lifestyle content. A monthly "In the Wind" section, which was a compilation of photos mailed in by readers and amateur chopper photographers, proved especially popular.

Month after month and, later, year by year, *Easyriders* and imitators including McMullen's *Chopper: The Real Biker Lifestyle, FTW Newsragazine*, and *Supercycle*, created by *Hustler* magazine's Larry Flynt, revealed for readers a full-bore chopper world. It was a place where the beer was always cold, the women young and willing, and the men all ready for a blast on their choppers or a punch-out at the local beer garden. Stereotypes that the magazines had hoped to transcend were later milked for their appeal to wannabe bikers. Cheesy fiction stories about big, bad righteous bikers

Launched as an offshoot of the popular Jammer's Handbook *chopper parts catalog,* Easyriders *magazine captured the chopper zeitgeist for a generation.*

Easyriders magazine

who invaded small towns, diddled the sheriff's daughter, and guzzled a case of Coors before thundering off into the sunset were integral parts of every issue. So were full-color centerfold paintings of bikers at play. Few could question the authenticity of the chopper magazines after they began running classified ads from biker gang members serving time in prisons and mail-order kits for manufacturing "speed and meth, cheap in your own homemade lab."

As outlandish and over the top as it seemed, the formula worked beyond anyone's estimation. Similar magazines were sprouting up across Europe and the United Kingdom by the mid-1980s, each offering readers an almost by-the-numbers guide to becoming an outlaw biker, replete with pedantic fiction and an endless array of photos from biker parties and runs.

The magazines had helped create the image of a Nietzschian Überbiker who represented the chopper lifestyle lived to its fullest. Readers could only hope to live up to the blueprint.

"There were only five copies of *Easyriders* available to our town in Italy when I was growing up in the late 1970s, and we'd all wait outside the store for two or three days to be first in line," said European chopper enthusiast and writer Giuseppe Roncen, who later formed *Freeway*, Italy's first chopper magazine. "We studied the magazines to build our own choppers, and guys would imitate the pictures when they formed their own outlaw chopper clubs."

The biker lifestyle magazines and the custom chopper builders enjoyed the perfect symbiotic relationship: Motorcycles featured in full-color articles would bring customers roaring into a builder's garage, for which they'd forever be indebted to the publishers, providing years of advertising revenue. In time, even magazines like *Cycle World* and the strictly sport bike–oriented *Motorcyclist* couldn't ignore the appeal of choppers and began, in the late 1990s, to feature the odd custom cruiser feature to their readers.

Clever editors at *Easyriders* were quick to capitalize on the appeal of their magazine's image, having been the first to lend each of the staff members listed in the masthead a made-for-Hollywood biker nickname. Some names like "Spider" and "Bandit" belied actual working staffers, while other perennials, such as the world's raunchiest "advice columnist" Miraculous Mutha, were inventions of the editors.

Easyriders wasted little time marketing biker lifestyle consumables to further codify the chopper experience. Hash pipes and T-shirts bearing cartoons of *Easyriders* staffers and logos were soon hawked side by side with chain wallets, swastika belt buckles, and, later, riding leathers and a Bros. Club motorcycle towing agency, much like an AAA for chopper riders. The centerfold models in today's chopper magazines now share the same plastic-enhanced Barbie doll aesthetic and the motorcycles are very often $100,000 rolling sculptures, seldom if ever ridden on the streets, but the magazines, now numbering in the dozens, still provide readers and chopper builders with a unique forum in which to study their art. McMullen, who died in 1988, would have been proud.

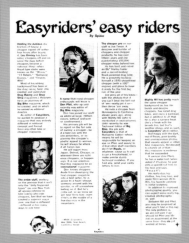

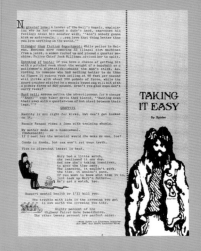

Lou "Spider" Kimzey, Joe Teresi, and Jammer Products CEO Mil Blair turned a garage hobby into a business empire.

Easyriders magazine

Rebirth and Rebuild

The Chopper is Reborn

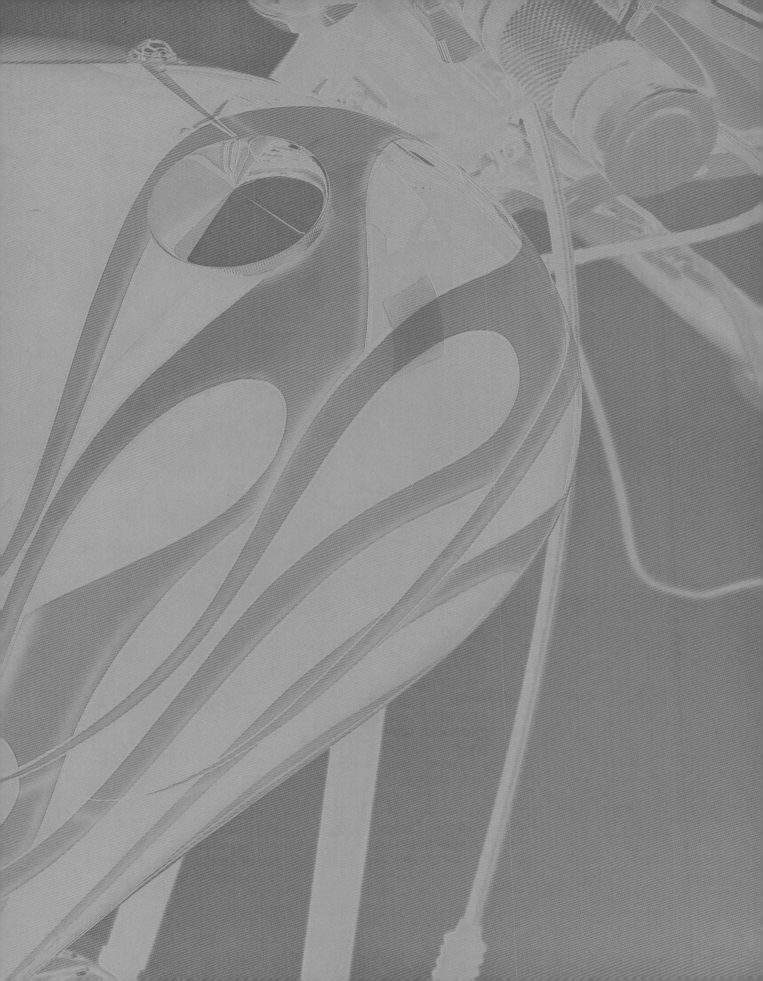

Jesse James' personal ride is
this stretched and raked
Evolution-powered chopper.
Anodized finishes highlight the
Ace of Spades air cleaner and
tough-as-nails knurled aluminum
handgrips. Mike Seate

During the height of the chopper craze, dozens of motorcycle-loving U.S. servicemen had taken to chopping their motorcycles while stationed at military installations around the globe. Some military personnel would build custom choppers at home where aftermarket parts were plentiful, and when a foreign assignment came along, they'd ship their raked-out lowriders to foreign posts for use as recreation and daily transportation. This is where overseas motorcyclists often got their first up-close look at this weird and rebellious new type of American bike. For many, choppers left a lasting impression.

Of course, Hollywood's biker movies had introduced the chopper to European and Asian audiences as early as 1966 when Roger Corman's homage to drugs and roadway nihilism, *The Wild Angels* was lauded by the European intellectual elite at the prestigious Venice International Film Festival as "a more realistic view of American youth" than Europeans had been accustomed to seeing in film and media. The fact that the outlaw chopper culture found a sympathetic ear in Europe so embarrassed the U.S. State Department that officials lobbied, unsuccessfully, to dissuade the film's producers from distributing *The Wild Angels* for a number of years.

Instead, American International Pictures pushed *The Wild Angels* and the studio's subsequent chopper movies to a willing worldwide audience, many of whom came away with a vision of building their own choppers, despite little knowledge of how to do so. In Europe there was almost a fetish for American cars and motorcycles that had been in effect since the closing days of WWII.

"When you talk with guys who've formed their own outlaw clubs or rode choppers in the early days [in Europe], most of them will tell you that they saw a biker movie and that's where they first saw choppers. Those movies were all exploitation, but they spread the chopper disease around," said Guiseppe Roncen, a chopper builder and founder of Freeway Publications, a European motorcycle magazine conglomerate based in Milan.

Turning what they'd seen on film or hanging around the local U.S. Army or Air Force base into a reality was a considerable challenge for a European chopper builder in those days. The aftermarket chopper parts craze that made building and maintaining a chopper as simple as choosing an item from a catalog and bolting it on for U.S. riders was virtually an unknown quantity in the rest of the world. But just like the early chopper builders learned in the United States, the lack of easy-to-find parts and accessories did little to deter foreign bike craftsmen from emulating their American idols when it came to chopping bikes.

Roncen said newspaper clippings from the Venice premiere of *Wild Angels* depicted a hearty pair of Italian bike enthusiasts riding obviously homemade Moto-Guzzi and Harley-Davidson choppers to the film.

The Scandinvavians led the way for the rest of Europe when it came to building choppers. Scandinavian custom builders had a long, proud history of mechanical expertise to draw from, evidenced by the high-end Volvo and Saab cars and aircraft manufactured by the Swedes. At an early age, many Swedish school students begin studying machine shop and metalworking skills, making for a culture with a strong tradesmen class in which the ability to craft metal into artistic objects is a source of national pride.

Many European countries had already embraced disparate elements from the 1960s drug culture, adopting everything from long hair to psychedelic drugs to love-ins and anti-Vietnam war protests. "From there, getting into American choppers was easy for them," Roncen said. So if the streets of Amsterdam or Brussels reflected the psychedelic culture of Southern California in dress, music, and culture, the outlaw chopper found easy acceptance in this socially liberal climate.

Chopper redux! Old stocks of Z-bars, peace-sign taillights, and other chopper regalia reappear in custom shops some three decades later. Mike Seate

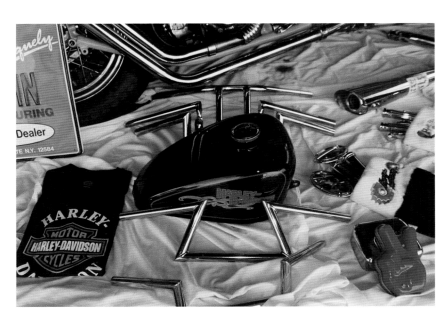

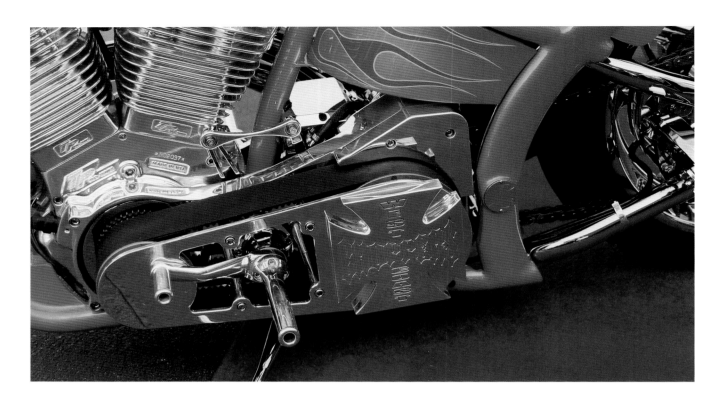

**Detail of an open-belt primary
drive on one of Jesse James'
El Diablo customs. James, like
many of today's top chopper
craftsmen, builds bikes made-
to-order but offers several
standard models as well. Note
Maltese-cross derby cover.**

Mike Seate

The chopper reached near icon status with Columbia Pictures' world-wide release of *Easy Rider* in 1970. European motorcyclists, who'd built a solid tradition of black leather and quick-throttled cafe racers, suddenly found themselves looking hopelessly outdated. Emulating championship racers like Mike Hailwood and John Surtees was suddenly yesterday's news. Choppers signaled that tuning in, turning on, and dropping out was now the key to two-wheeled enlightenment.

"Not for one single moment did we realize just what a significant and lasting impact *Easy Rider* would have on the British bike scene," wrote British chopper fanatic Maz Harris in his brilliant 1982 thesis on motorcy-cling, *Biker*. "Old-time rockers were growing their hair, wearing beads, and eagerly exploring the mind-bending properties of psychedelic drugs," he said. "British bikers formed themselves into loose-knit clubs, emulating their American precursors as best they could by sewing 'outlaw' patches onto their denims. . . . Nothing was ever the same again. Doing the ton down the bypass, chin on the tank, arse in the air, suddenly lost all its appeal. Now we rode our bikes along the high street, feet up and laid back, inviting the citizens to comment as we passed."

Harris, who became one of Britain's foremost academic chroniclers of the chopper subculture, helped form one of the UK's first outlaw bike gangs. He built and rode a series of choppers done up in the best mock-American style. But it was builders like Harris and, more passionately, the Swedish chopper aficionados, who managed to keep choppers alive when the U.S. bike scene had moved on to other, less antagonistic forms of two-wheeled transportation.

Growing up in the Northern Italian town of Vincenzia, Guiseppe Roncen remembers the infrequent but nonetheless eye-popping sight of a rare Swedish chopper on a run through Italy and became determined to build his own custom Harley. Made-in-Milwaukee motorcycles were scarce in Europe during the '60s and '70s, however, and many riders made do with whatever engines they could find.

British bikes, plentiful across the continent, formed the basis for many of Europe's first-generation stretch choppers, but with the exception of the Swedes and their famously high standard of living, new Harley-Davidsons were too expensive for the average fledgling easy rider.

As a result, a number of resourceful riders managed to unearth used Harley-Davidsons in the most unlikely places. "There were Swedish guys who were so determined to build an authentic Harley chopper they would travel to Belgium and buy police motorcycles or find old Military Flathead 45s left over from WWII," Roncen said. "There was a Harley importer in Italy

Ernie Daurham's "Assassin" breaks tradition with a thick, rubberized coating in place of paint. Built by John Covington at Arizona's Surgical Steeds, the bike is the chopper equivalent of a Stealth Bomber. Butch Lassiter, *IronWorks* magazine

back then, but he was only bringing in about 25 bikes a year because they were so costly." In Italy, riders would pool their resources and travel thousands of miles to North Africa to purchase used Harleys from Morocco's Royal Guard fleet at auction.

From there, it was all a matter of inventing choppers from scratch. For the Swedes, this was seldom a problem. Widely inspired by Peter Fonda's fabled red, white, and blue Panhead "Captain America," Swedish choppers quickly developed their trademark long and lean appearance. Born out of pure, unadulterated necessity and imagination, many of the Swedish chopper's signature components were mere stopgaps in their day. The 7-inch-wide, 15-inch rear wheels with 80 or more spokes seen on many European choppers (and widely imitated by American chopper builders today) came about as a result of mating chromed wire wheels from Jaguar and Ferrari sports cars to Harley-Davidson wheel hubs. Today, Swedish builders like Rogge Karlsson have taken the width and complexity of chopper wheels into truly mind-boggling territory, with rear wheels growing ever wider and front wheels narrowing by comparison.

The wicked, looped collector exhaust on the "Assassin." Twin Patrick Racing Mikuni carbs mean airflow through the 125-cubic-inch Axtell/STD motor is steady and fierce.

IronWorks magazine

The radically raked front forks, many 12 to 30 inches longer than stock, were often constructed on lathes in Sweden's many machine shops, while welding skills taught in schools came in handy for constructing hex and coffin gas tanks, cutting frame downtubes and raking steering heads. Some European builders became expert scavengers, utilizing the raked triple clamps from sidecar-equipped Triumph motorcycles for the additional 3 to 5 degrees of rake they offered.

Along with the twin inspirations of Hollywood biker exploitation films and the occasional chopper owned by a visiting U.S. serviceman was the rare

American chopper magazine. Unlike today, *Easyriders* didn't publish several foreign-language editions, and what few copies made it to Norway, Germany, Finland, or other chopper-mad countries were those of military personnel or the odd traveling biker. Roncen, who regularly waited for one of the five copies of *Easyriders* imported to his town's newsagent each month, said the chopper magazines offered their own share of inspiration for Europe's chopper fans.

"There were too many taxes on us if we tried to buy custom parts from the United States ourselves, so when a military guy you knew got a chopper catalog, you'd ask him to order things for you from his base. There are still loads of people over here doing it that way today," he says.

Not that the Europeans need to rely on the American chopper scene for much of anything anymore. At the most recent Daytona Beach Bike Week celebrations, European choppers wearing German, French, and even former Eastern Bloc license plates have rolled away with some of the most prestigious show trophies, and Roncen's custom Harley magazine, *Freeway,* routinely features radical choppers constructed from German frames, Italian forks, and Swedish suspension systems.

While U.S. riders were busy defending their rights to ride stretched and chopped machines back home, in Jarfalla, Sweden, legendary builder Torben "Tolle" Dehnisch had been building adjustable rake triple trees, stretched rigid frames, and other chopper components since 1979. With laws prohibiting ape-hanger handlebars and chopper forks surfacing in Great Britain and several other European countries, in 1983 the clever Tolle convinced authorities from Sweden's Road Traffic Institute of the structural integrity of his chopper forks and frames by volunteering his components for a series of 20 very demanding vehicle dynamics tests. Tolle's parts passed with flying colors, and by the mid-1980s, legislative restrictions against chopper building were rare in several European countries, Roncen said.

Dehnisch managed to reveal the hypocrisy and ignorance of the safety officials, who seemed to have simply plucked their restrictions figures limiting choppers to 35 degrees of rake or 5-cubic-inch-over-stock forks from thin air. In the end, Tolle continued to build choppers to his highly exacting standards. He even enlisted the help of Sweden's Royal Technical High School in testing the aircraft-quality alloys he used to construct his fork parts.

"I really think [the Europeans] kept the chopper thing alive when it had all but died in the States. The myth and mystique of riding a chopper never died down, especially in Sweden," said Roncen.

The gas tank may be Harley-Davidson stock, but this oddball chopper's motor started life aboard a Yamaha Radian 500 sport bike. British and European chopper builders have learned to make do with what's available.
Mike Seate

Bikes like this stroker from Canada's Rumble Customs combine longbike looks with near superbike performance. Collector exhaust canisters and low-profile rear rubber are straight out of the racing paddock. Paul Martinez

Roncen's observation that choppers were more popular in Europe for a time than in their native United States rings true, but there were always a few longbikes to be found on America's highways, even during the 1980s. Some were built and ridden by hard-core chopper devotees who simply refused to change bikes to suit the times, while elaborate show bikes sporting extended springers and old-school mural paint jobs were always a staple of the custom bike show circuit. And, as reflected by today's new crop of custom builders, choppers had started creating a swell of interest among youthful biking enthusiasts, most of whom were too young to remember the chopper from its heyday but were nonetheless attracted to its style.

In recent years, the unbridled growth of the World Wide Web has help spread the chopper gospel, with new online biker magazines and chopper worship sites springing up every month. Two of the more successful and comprehensive chopper websites belong to "Chopper" Dave Freston of Burbank, California (www.chopperdaves.com), and Guy Bolton of greasykulture.com fame, a native of London now living and riding in Sydney, Australia.

With the science of frame geometry and suspension sussed, builders are exploring unheard-of fork lengths and frame dimensions while still maintaining rideability.

Paul Martinez

Freston's popular website is long on historical photos and, like the lifestyle magazines of the 1970s, provides back-alley chopper builders with a public forum to display their work.

Still in his early 30s, Freston is at the vanguard of the West Coast's retro-chopper scene, where youthful '50s and '60s revisionists not only build replicas of the "bob job" motorcycles from the early postwar era but dress the part as well. The scene gathers several times annually at places like the Viva Las Vegas Rockabilly Weekender, a celebration of hot rods, chopper culture, and hepcat music, or England's Hemsby Festival, where, to the untrained eye, it appears visitors have wandered into a time warp, pompadours, poodle skirts, and all.

Bolton, 37, shares Freston's devotion to nostalgia and classic American street style, whether it be the pop and roar of an unmuffled Harley-Davidson motor, the sinewy lines of a chopped Triumph Bonneville, or the timeless cool of black leather and engineer boots.

Bolton admits to being drawn to choppers through American biker movies in his childhood, then spending the next two decades and several thousand dollars trying to replicate the movie machines in his backyard London shed. "For me, interest in American motorcycles and outlaw culture of the '40s to the '60s stemmed from a love of everything else from those periods: music, clothes, architecture art and literature," Bolton said. "I think the resurgence of choppers is part of a backlash against the high-tech, plastic-packaged

Indian Larry, one of the East Coast's better-known chopper builders, practicing his craft.
Guiseppi Roncen

Opposite page
Larger displacement engines producing well over 120 rear-wheel horsepower are only appearing in choppers through recent developments in frame construction. Roger Bourget of Arizona's Bourget's Bike Works was among the first to weld and design his own chassis. Modern thick-walled and structurally sound frames make bends and stress fractures things of the past.
Paul Martinez

Indian Larry on his rigid Panhead. Mustang tank harkens back to the earliest days of chopping when tanks from Mustang and Cushman scooters were pressed into chopper duty. The adjustable steering damper is there for Larry's frequent forays into stunt riding. Guiseppi Roncen

society the Western world has become. Nowadays it's almost impossible to rebel: Parents and cops have seen it all before and are shocked by nothing. Anyone can jump on a Kawasaki Ninja and go fast, but more and more people are discovering it's more challenging, dangerous, rebellious and cool to go fast on a contraption you built yourself that was designed to go slow."

The similarities between these postmoderns and the chopper riders of the 1960s is striking: As motorcycles grow faster, lighter, and more technologically complex, a group of anti-modernists look to the chopper for a reprieve from what the manufacturers are selling. Chopper revisionists like Bolton go back a long way in Europe, where American pop culture has always had its fanatical devotees.

For example, in the late 1970s, West Coast builder Denver Mullins of Denver's Choppers fame responded to correspondence from a Swedish chopper club, accepting an invitation to an international bike show. "He came over and started a shop in Stockholm, and pretty soon he met a club of chopper riders who wanted to name their club Denver's in his honor. They all rode choppers with at least 20-inches-over front forks and no front brakes and only suicide shifts and ape-hangers. They were dedicated," *Freeway*'s Roncen said.

Of course, there's nowhere like home, and by the time Roncen's *Free-way* magazine was up and covering the burgeoning European biker show and party circuit in 1994, he had also become a regular feature of American biker gatherings where a new generation of U.S. chopper builders were starting to emerge. The U.S. aftermarket was being spurred this time by a unique reality of a booming economy. Harley-Davidson Motor Co., which had fared so poorly during the 1970s under the corporate leadership of American Machine Foundry (AMF), was now producing handsome, oil-tight, reliable motorcycles. The public had come around to appreciating the Milwaukee firm's accomplishments as a genuine American success story, and by 1994 Harley-Davidson couldn't produce their air-cooled V-twin motorcycles fast enough to meet demand.

With customers forced to sign their names to waiting lists for months and, in some cases, years to purchase one of the suddenly fashionable Hogs, parts manufacturers from across the country responded by launching dozens of Harley-Davidson clone bikes, crafted entirely from aftermarket parts. Mostly reflecting the current popularity of fat-tanked, low-slung cruisers with shortened forks and luxury amenities like air-glide, softail suspension systems, the clone bikes offered an expensive, upscale take on the hand-built custom motorcycle. The quality of these clones varied widely from builder to builder, with some builders producing factory-quality custom bikes and others building machines that were not much better than a backyard amateur's home-brewed chopper. The aftermarket assembly houses did include several choppers in their lineups, with California Motorcycle Company and, later, Panzer, a Colorado outfit specializing in neoclassic Panhead motors, assembling road-worthy replicas of the famed Captain America and Billy choppers from the movie *Easy Rider*.

Though the hand-built motorcycles from Titan, Big Dog, Ultra, and dozens of others sold briskly at anywhere from $20,000 to $60,000 each,

Bobber cruisin' European style. Like Civil War reenactors, European chopper riders are sticklers for period detail. Note the jockey shift, white silk scarf, and missing front fenders—very 1950s! Guiseppi Roncen

The look is pure California, but the location is Norway, site of the Harley-Davidson Super Rally. Shotgun drag pipes a foot longer than this rigid Panhead leave a lasting impression.

Guiseppi Roncen

many youthful custom motorcycle enthusiasts were turned off by the pastel-colored luxury cruisers offered by the Harley alternative market.

Some, like Arizona's Paul Yaffee and the moody, Mohawk-wearing Roger Bourget, remembered an era of custom motorcycles in which less was more and set out to recreate the spare, laid-back bikes of their childhoods, with a decidedly modern technological flair.

Bourget's Bike Works, located just outside sunny Phoenix, Arizona, has become a standout from the aftermarket assembly scene for taking orders for a line of 12 different bikes that are choppers in the purest sense of the word. The rigid Low Blow frames offer a unique oil-in-chassis design and a pavement-scraping 19-inch seat height. Bourget seems unafraid to challenge conventional thought concerning fork length and paint scheme. As has become standard among today's postmodern chopper builders, Bourget favors growling, drag strip–ready power plants in his bikes, with 96- and 113-cubic-inch aftermarket motors from S&S Cycle a common choice. These motors supply levels of horsepower that would easily bend or twist the frame tubing on early chopper frames, but through liberal use of chrome-moly tubing on frames and chassis designs that utilize fewer long areas of tubing, the current generation of choppers can more than handle the whopping 80 and 90 foot-pounds of torque these engines offer.

Another Arizonan taking full advantage of technological advantages available to modern chopper building is Paul Yaffee. Born in San Fernando Valley, California, the boyish, clean-shaven Yaffee attended mechanics classes at the American Motorcycle Institute before turning his skills into a World's Most Beautiful Motorcycle award at the hallowed Oakland (California) Roadster Show for three years running between 1998 and 2000. From there, Yaffee took his extensive experience working with billet aluminum to market with his Paul Yaffee Originals line of high-end custom components and complete made-to-order choppers.

Blessed with a mathematician's eye for creating exacting steering geometry, Yaffee is a big proponent of creating choppers that look every bit as spindly and hard to ride as their 1960s counterparts

High-tunnel gas tank and over 40 degrees of rake make for a seriously low-profile chopper seen rolling across the judges' stand at the Swedish Harley-Davidson Super Rally, 2001. Note the youthful age of the "judges."

Guiseppi Roncen

but are actually sheep in wolves clothing out on the highway. "If you get the trail measurements correct, a stretch chopper can handle just as good in a tight circle or a parking lot as it does out on the highway. A lot of the old guys just experimented with rake and fork length, but if you study the dimensions right, it really works and doesn't have to be slow steering," said Yaffee, who, like many of today's celebrity chopper builders, utilized the latest computer software and design technology to create flawless choppers.

Flawless is also a great way to describe the choppers emerging from the Florida workshop of French expatriate Cyril Huze. Painstaking in their detail and refinement, Huze spends months designing and building each component of his luxury choppers, motorcycles that have been described as "renaissance art on two wheels." Rich with art-deco influences, pop-art murals, and elegant metalwork that would not appear out of place on a vintage Rolls Royce, Huze has taken the chopper places where many never imagined it would go.

Picking up where the chopper aftermarket left off a generation before, builders like Big Mike Rouse, manufacturer of the BMC line of choppers, started offering customers mail-order choppers in 1997.

Genuine Harley-Davidson motors were in short supply when Europe caught the chopper bug. This Volkswagen car engine in a trike frame proves how ingenious and resourceful these builders were.

Guiseppi Roncen

When the idea first occurred to Rouse, he remembers being told there's no way a mass-manufactured rigid-frame motorcycle would find an audience. By the time Rouse brought his first prototype to Myrtle Beach Bike Week in 1997, however, he'd secured 300 orders for his "Notorious" choppers. Today, Rouse produces about 25 bikes each month from his Orange County headquarters, each infused with his bare-knuckle styling and early '60s-style Friscoed Sportster gas tanks. "The classic choppers all had Sporty gas tanks, rigid frames, and big, open pipes. I was determined to bring that styling back, but this time using top-of-the-line parts and motors that would last," said Rouse, who favors 100-cubic-inch Rev Tech power plants, or Harley's new vibration-free Twin Cam 88B.

Chopper-riding U.S. military personnel provided many European riders with their first real contact with custom bikes. These mid-1970s French riders seem to be quick studies.

Guiseppi Roncen

Being relatively younger than many of his competitors, Rouse is fully aware of how the costs of building or buying a chopper have grown since the stretchbikes came back into style. With the wallet-challenged in mind, he started marketing complete, running BMC choppers with payment and financing plans that can suit even the poorest easy rider. "I know what it's like to want a cool bike and have just a little money," he says.

Alongside the dense field of talented newcomers like Billy Lane of Florida's Choppers Inc. and the legendary Jesse James are some salty veterans who've adapted their timeless chopper stylings to the modern era. In Oakland, California, Ron Simms has launched a line of heavyweight customs under the ominous Thugg title; they are wide, ghetto-fabulous machines that are aesthetically linked to inner-city hip-hop styles and lowrider cars. Simms, who has seen choppers come and go out of fashion several times, still crafts a mean stretch chopper and maintains his ability to build either long or low bikes with equal aplomb.

Frame molding and spray-gun wizard Mondo Porras at Henderson, Nevada's, Denver's Choppers has refused to compete with the fat-bike builders and remains true to his roots, continuing to build stretch choppers that demand attention—and a lot of turning room.

Denver's current catalog of choppers, to the untrained eye, is barely discernible from the outlaw longbikes that once cruised around its West Coast garage. Only the price tags and levels of technical accomplishment would put starch in a '60s' rebel's ponytail. "I never went in for that shortened-forks and wide-tanks look. I always thought choppers should be long and lean and have as few extra parts on 'em as possible. A chopper is supposed to be the kind of bike that people can't help but stare at and think *Damn! Now that's something!*" Porras said.

Porras has no plans to retire anytime soon, and he's the first to admit that the last 40 years in the chopper business have been a wild, unpredictable ride in an industry that, even in its heyday, didn't exactly smack of long-term job security. But to see a new generation of mechanical craftsmen embrace the designs, ideas, and attitudes that he and men of his time made into icons is a reward that few of the original chopper builders ever could have imagined.

"This has all come a long way in the last 40 years. I like seeing the young guys coming along like Billy Lane and Jesse [James]. I wish Denver [Mullins] could have lived to see the gleam in their eyes when they talk about the kinds of choppers they like to build, because it's just like what he and I used to have," he said. "These new choppers are all about clean, smooth-flowing lines and big, kick-ass motors and none of the bolt-on crap. I never thought I'd see this come back again, but I'm glad to see it."

Two decades in business have helped Pat Kennedy master the art of longbike design. Wild murals, wide, easy-to-control handlebars, and Byzantine arrays of twisted spoke wheels are Kennedy classics. Paul Martinez

A Gallery of Choppers
and Builders

Chapter 5

From the Ground Up

COOL MAGAZINE

Freeway

FREEWAY - DICEMBRE 2000 N° **81**
HARLEY, CHOPPER & CUSTOM

L. 8500

FREEWAY

YAM CHOP • HERITAGE EFI 2001

RADUNI: HCS BOLZANO, GRIFONI ETNA, STONE COLD

diabolico
West Coast Chopper
El Borracho!

dossier
HARDCORE
custom estremo
secondo Marcus Walz

In addition to introducing a wealth of new ideas and unique visions to the reborn art of chopper building, today's new school of custom craftsmen have adapted computer-age technology to the streets. Computer-assisted drafting allows custom wheels to be designed in cyberspace and tested for structural soundness and durability long before the first mile is turned out on the highway. Billet aluminum, that is, massive, solid chunks of alloy that are milled into chopper parts, also caused a revolution in the custom motorcycle industry, permitting the sorts of structural integrity and torsional rigidity previously employed only by the aerospace industry.

Chopped, in the twenty-first century, no longer means unsafe, unsteady, or jury-rigged; advances in welding techniques and metallurgical engineering have created chopper frames manufactured from thick, stress-resistant chrome-moly steel. With downtubes measuring 1-3/8 inches in diameter, even the heftiest stroker motor can't torque one of these chassis out of shape. Handlebar wiring has grown invisi-

James, long a popular figure in chopper magazines like **Easyriders** *and Italy's* **Freeway,** *has crossed into the cultural mainstream. In December 2002 he was selected as one of* **People** *magazine's "Sexiest Men Alive."* Guiseppe Roncen

Previous pages
New tire technology allows chopper builders to mount massive read rubber up to 10 inches in width. Paul Martinez

ble due to clever internal wiring systems, while oil tanks and entire big twin motors are commonly rubber-mounted to reduce vibration. Aftermarket frames are manufactured today with welds and tabs mostly smoothed over, reducing the need for molding and extensive bodywork. And kick starters, the chopper rider's Achilles' heel, have largely been consigned to the easily forgotten past.

Softail frames with air-adjustable suspension systems are evening out road irregularities that once had a generation of chopper riders crying for their kidney belts, while custom bike builders like Pure Steel's John Covington now offer progressive fork-damping units on their road race–style upside-down cartridge chopper forks, permitting a level of performance that chopper builders of the 1960s and '70s couldn't have imagined.

While thousands of backyard chopper parts suppliers have faded away over the years, some of the old-school veterans who cut their creative teeth on king and queen seats and peace-sign sissy bars have adapted to the changing times and updated their custom offerings to suit today's more demanding chopper enthusiast. Aftermarket powerhouses Paughco, Drag Specialties, Arlen Ness, and Mid-USA, to name but a few, are now pumping out chopper accessories bereft of the hit-or-miss quality that plagued choppers a few decades earlier.

"Lots of guys built their own chopper parts from scratch, because back in the old days, you never really knew whether what you were buying mail-order was good quality or whether the guy with the little magazine ad could actually do better than you could with a hacksaw and a welding torch," said North Carolina chopper wizard Rick Doss.

Doss, who today manufactures made-to-order choppers imbued with the high-end build quality and uncompromising performance of classic Italian sports cars, is typical of the new breed of chopper builders who blend imagination and technology into unforgettable pieces of rolling art.

Nearly outlawed in the 1970s, choppers may have been forced underground, but the scrutiny under which safety officials placed them only seems

Pay up, suckers! Jesse James' backpiece tattoo means business. Mike Seate

Jesse James on the road to Sturgis aboard his Camel Roadhouse stroker.
Guiseppe Roncen

Bikes like this sassy Evolution chopper, built as a promotion for Camel cigarettes, have placed Jesse James' name on the lips of millions of bikers.

to have helped choppers to reemerge better, stronger, faster, and, ultimately, way cooler than before.

Jesse James—Outlaw for Hire

At a time when most twenty-something men were busy dreaming of souped-up Mustangs and fluorescent green Kawasaki Ninjas, Jesse James obsessed about old school choppers. I first met Jesse in the early 1990s when both of us were working security details for underground rock bands. As a weightlifter and former college football player for the University of California at Riverside, Jesse made a perfect bodyguard. Between sets at the clubs, Jesse busied himself talking about designs for custom motorcycles, a task he seemed to take to with almost child-like enthusiasm. None of us thought much of this young dreamer's lofty intentions back then. Most of us had our own get-rich-quick schemes or unrealized plans for car and motorcycle shops.

But when Jesse, a native of his beloved Long Beach, California, began crafting hand-made motorcycle parts in his mother's garage a few years later, it was worth noting. Instead of simply mimicking the wide, low Fatbob bikes popular at the time, Jesse's first forays into custom bike building revealed a vision strictly out of left field. Lush, padded seats as wide as a La-Z Boy recliner were nowhere to be found. Also absent were floorboards, fringe, and other pretensions to the genteel Harleys popular in the 1950s. Instead, Jesse's first custom bike was a wickedly-fast 93 cubic inch Pan/Shovel combo. He quickly followed that machine with several more choppers including a mean, sleek, black rigid-framed Shovelhead, an exercise in minimalism. Black orange flames and infused with a muscular purposeful look, the rigid Shovel featured hand-made steel fenders and a seat that was scarcely more than a hand-pounded aluminum pan. An eight-inch-over Wide Glide front fork with flat drag bars and shotgun pipes completed Jesse's early custom, which I wrote up in the pages of the now-defunct New York custom chopper magazine, *Iron Horse*.

The first ground-up custom to emerge from West Coast Choppers was this rigid black Shovelhead. Author

"What do you guys think?" he asked. I told Jesse that if this was any indication of his future, he'd do quite well.

Jesse didn't instantly rocket to the top of the custom chopper trade, despite the

worldwide acclaim that he's experienced in recent years. For two years, he continued to build and design his bikes—mostly in his mind—while he worked at his day job designing components for aftermarket parts manufacturer Performance Machine and later, for hot rod car magnate Boyd Coddington.

Frustrated by crafting other people's ideas into reality (and cash), Jesse doggedly learned the sheetmetal worker's craft. In his spare time he taught himself to manipulate old school tools like the English wheel, a sheetmetal manipulating device capable of making convex and concave shapes out of flat steel. He studied metal crafting under a New England master skilled at using the old power hammers and metal-shrinking machines used to manufacture airplanes during WWII.

Jesse spent long nights learning to weld with seamless precision and studying newfangled devices like CNC machining systems and computer-assisted drafting.

He wasn't just spinning his wheels. Jesse knew that in order to re-invent the chopped Harleys that had wowed him as a kid, he'd need to master every aspect of bike building. "I always thought a lot of the stuff on the (aftermarket chopper parts) scene was crap," he said. "The craftsmanship

Young chopper builders like Jesse James of West Coast Choppers have rejuvenated the chopper scene in the United States.

Guiseppe Roncen

was shit and most of it either wouldn't fit straight up to somebody's bike, or it was cheap and would vibrate apart once you got it out on the road. I'd go to Daytona or the Oakland Roadster Show and see what everybody else was making. I knew my stuff was better looking."

Jesse may have been cocky, but he had the skills to back up his bravado.

He never lacked for influences. From childhood, Jesse had been constantly exposed to the Latino lowrider culture that was an integral part of the Long Beach scene. His father Larry James was a custom car enthusiast as well. As a kid, outlaw bike gangs often blasted by the family car, the flash of chrome and the roar of unmuffled pipes making a lasting impression on the young Jesse.

While West Coast Choppers was still a cottage industry operating out of a tiny garage, Jesse become a fan of the Los Angeles hip-hop scene, where inner-city style had turned the classic lowriders and hot rods into over-the-top representations of urban machismo and flash style.

All of these disparate influences percolated inside James' head while he worked in his home shop. By the early 1990s, Jesse began formulating the edgy, post-industrial fenders, gas tanks, and entire motorcycles that fill his catalog today. Even then, it took a while before anyone listened. Meetings with bigwigs from the motorcycle customizing aftermarket would often end with Jesse leaving dejectedly. He was told again and again that his ideas

Paul Yaffee working on one of his original creations. Dain Gingerelli

were "too way out" or that choppers were out of style and that they'd never make a comeback.

"Everywhere I went it was like, 'people are into fat bikes, period,'" he recalls. "Then they'd take a good long look at my shit and show me the door."

But Jesse had a mentor in Ted Pardee, a neighbor from his old Ventura neighborhood who built some of the fastest top fuel Sportsters ever to burn up a Southern Californian quarter-mile. "Ted was really cool," Jesse said.

From the hidden axle adjusters to the collector exhaust system and 10-inch-wide rear fender, Yaffee's "Bad to the Bone" is all attitude all the time. Butch Lassiter, *Ironworks* magazine

The big-inch power plants Yaffee uses in his customs are not your grandfather's Evos. Butch Lassiter, *Ironworks* magazine

"He built these Sportsters that were so stripped down they looked like dirt bikes, but they were fast as hell. He really opened my eyes to the idea of building what you like and following your own vision rather than trying to do what everybody else was doing just to make a buck."

With nothing more than a notebook full of ideas and a low tolerance for bullshit, Jesse parted ways with Coddington in 1994, setting out to launch West Coast Choppers as a place where his visions would either sink or swim.

They swam, all right. Like a shark on steroids.

When asked recently why his choppers have proven so popular, why a custom motorcycle builder still in his 30s has almost single-handedly re-launched choppers on the international scene, Jesse just shrugged. "I really try to get into people's heads when I build a bike for them. I try and get into everything from the kind of music they listen to, to how they dress and who they are."

The ability to evoke a customer's personality in a motorcycle design has been one of the major factors in West Coast's popularity with the celebrity set. Basketball star Shaquille O'Neil, professional wrestler Steve Goldberg, and supermodel Tyson Beckford have all visited the Aneheim Avenue workshop for "fittings" for their new bikes. Though busy operating a huge mail-order parts business and international retail outlets in Europe, Jesse sets aside a few days to get to know his customers and their riding styles. This way, he produces a ground-up custom bike in the same way an artist renders a portrait.

French expatriate, design guru, and high-concept chopper artist Cyril Huze. Mike Seate

There's a strong sense of playfulness, irreverence, and good old fashioned mischief in Jesse's choppers, evidenced in ideas like the One Ton Ho fenders, named after Long Beach slang for "a really, really healthy girl." His gas tanks are still hand-formed from flat steel, a labor-intensive process that produces bikes with the voluptuousness of a young Jane Russell.

West Coast's patented three-dimensional Maltese cross air cleaners are intended as a send-up of the wacky Maltese cross taillights and rear-view mirrors of the 1960s. West Coast customs tend to be designed for the ultimate in street visibility and notice-me cool. The Hell Bent exhaust system, for instance, which features a set of wickedly curved, variable-diameter open drag pipes, amplify the already boisterous noise of a stroker motor to near airport-runway levels. The popular CFL or Choppers For Life rigid frames are still hand-made like all West Coast chassis', and the detail is simply breathtaking. The low-slung frame positions a rider just inches from the rushing pavement, while the matching 38 degree rake and four-inch stretch places a rider's hands in a high, extended position. But Jesse has designed these bikes to be every-day rideable—he's piloted his own CFL from Long Beach to Sturgis, South Dakota and back.

Not that we're talking two-wheeled lawn chairs here. Knurled handgrips, suicide shifters, and narrow hand-stitched seats are common at West Coast, as are monster V-Twin motors from the likes of S&S, Patrick Racing, and Merch Performance, many boasting displacements well over 100 cubic inches. At full throttle they can be unsettling, ballsy beasts that require an expert rider who's not afraid to cause commotion.

James was one of the first chopper builders to experiment with the ultra-wide 200- and 240-mm rear tires. He found that by widening the rear sections of his Dragon Softail frames and fashioning transmission offsets to accommodate chain final drives instead of belts, these hyper-rubbers could be run with ease. Handmade round aluminum oil tanks bearing the etched CFL logo have also become a must-have West Coast signature piece, inspired by the hex-shaped oil bags often seen on original choppers from the '70s. James has recently begun experimenting with odd textures and chemical finishes on some components. Chromic Acid etching on foot pegs and fork lowers, for instance is a finish formerly utilized in military aircraft and vehicles. This finish leaves a thick, almost plastic-looking appearance over metals. It's just another way James has managed to stay ahead of a burgeoning and highly talented field.

Though a few long bikes have rolled out of the Jesse James garage, and the radically stretched and raked Villain model is long enough to give even Shaq room to stretch out, most West Coast project bikes are borne with relatively conservative fork lengths. "There's nothing that can beat a longbike for just cruisin' but I like a bike to still be fast and handle so that you can whip it around if you need to," Jesse explains.

If asked which West Coast Choppers custom parts has sold the most units, Jesse will laugh and say, "The T-shirts." In the wake of Motorcycle Mania, a popular TV special that aired on cable's Discovery Channel in late 2000, Jesse found himself unprepared for the onrush of publicity and serious money he was in for. Motorcycle Mania provided a human look at a driven young entrepreneur, warts and all. Capturing the West Coast crew as they

Evoking the graceful, sculpted elegance of classic touring cars and art deco architecture, Cyril Huze choppers are more High Street than back alley.

Mike Seate

strained and struggled to meet an impossible deadline before the annual Camel Roadhouse custom bike show at Daytona Beach Bike Week, it managed to make a celebrity out of someone who was only doing his job.

The phones seldom stopped ringing after the show aired, and an expanding catalog of T-shirts, jackets, hats, and other chopper ephemera soon grew even larger as thousands of chopper fans suddenly wanted to not only ride West Coast style, but dress the part too.

With the original program acknowledged as one of Discovery Network's highest rated shows ever, a second installment, Motorcycle Mania II, followed in early 2002. The spirited documentary following Jesse and several other chopper builders riding from Long Beach to Sturgis, South Dakota for the annual Sturgis Rally and Races, again proved popular. It also illustrated how far the chopper movement had come in American society in just 30 years. It's impossible to imagine Big Daddy Roth receiving prime-time coverage for a leisure trip with a few riding buddies.

Best of all, viewers were actually given the chance to win a complete West Coast Chopper through a network sweep-

Chromed, 80-spoke wheels may have their origins in the "whatever works" European chopper scene, but Bourget's has turned wire wheels into high art.

Paul Martinez

stakes. The staff at West Coast Choppers had since grown to over 20, while Jesse's own eclectic stable of toys grew to include a 260 horsepower Suzuki Hayabusa superbike, a Ducati 996, a Dodge Viper, several vintage hot rods, and, of course, several choppers. Late in 2002, The Discovery Channel gave birth to its first genuine star as Jesse was chosen to host "Monster Garage" a wild, post-industrial weekly series in which Jesse leads a team of hand-picked welders, designers, and mechanics on a seven-day quest to transform everyday cars, trucks, and service vehicles into multi-purpose customs.

The idea of changing a Volkswagen Beetle into a floating, fully operational Louisiana swamp buggy, a Mini Cooper into a tracked snowmobile, and a school bus into a pontoon boat caught the public's attention in ways that Jesse might never have imagined. By the close of it's first season, "Monster Garage" was pulling in 2 million viewers each week and posting its hard-working star in the pages of Gentleman's Quarterly, People, and the New York Times.

Captain America revisited? Paul Martinez

Jesse will tell you that the quick flight to the top has been strange and puzzling at times. It generally takes less than a month for knock-offs of some of his more innovative inventions to show up on other custom bikes. During their annual visits to Daytona Bike Week, the West Coast crew resembled stunned patent attorneys as they uncovered hundreds of imitation West Coast

Exile Cycle's Russ Mitchell, a London veterinarian turned chopper builder, will paint a motorcycle any color you want, as long as it's black.

Dain Gingerelli

parts and garments for sale at vendor booths. Shops advertising custom built choppers with logos and imagery similar to that of West Coast can be found in most towns these days, testament to Jesse's influence and the ruthless competitiveness of today's chopper scene.

Keeping it real has never seemed tougher at West Coast, but Jesse insists on staying connected to the streets, where he'd been himself just a few

Computer-aided drafting has helped builders like Arizona's Roger Bourget create elaborate wheel designs. Paul Martinez

Billet aluminum calipers and drilled brake rotors are standard fare on modern choppers. Knee-deep Imron paint can add a good four figures to the cost of a custom bike. Paul Martinez

years earlier. With choppers now catching on with a younger generation of custom motorcycle enthusiasts, he finds that these guys who are long on ideas and low on cash really appreciate talking directly to the guy who designed their bike's parts. "Some of the young guys may not have $3,000 to invest in a set of wheels or $1,200 for a gas tank, maybe they can just afford one part or two. But they're so into it. They just want to ride a really bitchin' bike and they really appreciate being able to come up to you at a rally and talk."

Paul Yaffee: Steel Driving Man

Like legendary railroad laborer John Henry, California native Paul Yaffee came into the chopper trade in the early 1990s swinging a hammer for all he was worth. A self-taught sheet-metal craftsman with a degree from Arizona's American Motorcycle Institute, Yaffee was determined to bring originality to the chopper scene. After winning the prestigious Grand National Roadster Show in Oakland, California, for three years running, Yaffee set up shop in arid Phoenix, Arizona, and began seriously designing a line of parts and complete chopped motorcycles. His line of Paul Yaffee Originals, noted for the sleek, flowing lines and gracefully arching frame contours, has garnered him countless show trophies, magazine coverage, and the sort of international stardom that used to be reserved for rock musicians and actors. Not afraid to break convention, Yaffee has taken the longbike look to new, ever-lengthening dimensions. Rakes of 50 and even 60 degrees are not unknown on Yaffee choppers, but he swears by his machine's handling prowess due to a deep understanding of frame geometry and rake and trail dimensions.

Yaffee says he eliminated front-end "flop," or that heavy, one-sided feel associated with many early stretch choppers, through perfect measurement of trail.

In layman's terms, we're talking about a chopper that can blast through a snaky canyon road and a board-straight piece of blacktop with equal ease. In a word: original.

Billy Lane: Southern Fried Engineering

At Melbourne, Florida's, Choppers Inc., youthful proprietor Billy Lane has an approach to building choppers that could be described as playful or even irreverent. Instead of following conventional ideas about what a chopper should look like or how it should perform, Lane seems to follow only his own lead. A master of utilizing found materials in his wildly detailed concept bikes, you're as likely to see a grill from a 1920s Ford Model A as an aftermarket springer fork on one of Lane's bikes. His long list of innovations in the chopper field include the much-imitated, six-shooter handlebar riser caps—inlaid with genuine 9-mm brass cartridge ends—wicked Devil's-tail plug-wire covers and a free-floating rear-wheel mounting kit with a single-sided swing-arm. Featured in an episode of cable TV's *Motorcycle Mania* series, Lane revealed how he peruses flea markets, antiques shows, and swap meets in his ceaseless search for unusual items that can be used to create

Following pages
Billy Lane brings everything including the kitchen sink to his wild and wacky choppers—note the faucet-handle shifter knob and leaf-spring front forks.

Mark Langello, *IronWorks* magazine

Kjell (left) and Joel of Choppers Unlimited, located in Guadalajara, Mexico, have merged high-concept European chopper style and back-alley grit for some badass results. Paul Martinez

Choppers Unlimited makes the most of Mexico's famously lenient vehicle-design restrictions and creates some truly mind-blowing custom bikes. Note how the ubiquitous disc brakes seen on Stateside choppers are nonexistent south of the border. Paul Martinez

an unforgettable chopper. A spare rear cylinder for a Harley Shovelhead motor, for example, found its way into a chopper that Lane built using two rear jugs and a one-off left-side collector exhaust system. For a builder relatively new to the game, Lane's hand-pounded steel peanut gas tank, often adorned with vintage pin-up art, and his tractor-wide rear tires on narrow, wasp-waisted rigid-framed choppers have become as recognizable as the lumpy idle of a stroked big twin.

Russ Mitchell: Exile On Main Street

Russ Mitchell's relocation from rainy England to Southern California didn't affect the eccentric Brits's eye for mean street choppers. Mitchell, a former wildlife veterinarian who wears a flaming red Mohawk and colorful Hawaiian shirts, prefers that choppers follow three basic design rules: They have to be black, they have to be fast, and they have to be basic. "In England, bikes are tough, rough, bad, mean, and noisy, and there's nothing nice about them. That's what I want to capture with my choppers. I want nothing to do with decorating, and I don't want to see turn signals, mirrors, taillights, and senseless add-ons," he said. And you won't: Exile choppers are cut down to custom motorcycling's base essentials and offer a look that's about as subtle as a sawed-off shotgun. Most start with a 120-cubic-inch Keck billet motor thumping out horsepower on the far side of 120; open primaries with Karata 4-inch exposed belt drives; tiny solo saddles; fat, barely covered tires on both ends; stretched one-piece tanks with nary an instrument in sight; and plenty of moody black paint. "There's nothing cute going on here," Mitchell says.

Cyril Huze: Chopper as an Art Form

Where many of his contemporaries are approaching choppers with an eye for toughness and raw, street-smart looks, French-born Cyril Huze builds

Freeway *magazine's* Guiseppe Roncen *travels across the country on his way to Sturgis with Indian Larry and* Jesse James *in* Motorcycle Mania II. Guiseppe Roncen

Father and son team Pat and Cole Foster of Salinas Boyz Customs created this twenty-first century interpretation of the classic bobber. Guiseppe Roncen

choppers that are not afraid to embrace elegance and sophistication. Painstaking in their detail, Huze builds only 10 or so complete, ground-up customs each year, allowing himself time to invest hundreds of hours designing each component. Editors have likened the gracefully voluptuous bikes to the luxury touring sedans of pre-Depression America, and they're not far from the mark: Art-deco design elements are evident in the elongated Huze gas tanks and flowing lines of his wrap-around oil tanks that segue seamlessly into his chassis. Pointed, crescent moon-shaped fenders and pastel paint schemes are proof that Huze, who studied the chopper scene for years before building his first custom, is a builder following his own vision.

Bourget's Bike Works: Southwest Steel

Arizona's chopper renaissance has produced more talented builders than you can shake a sissy bar at, but few are more respected than Roger Bourget. An admitted workaholic who insists that his choppers perform as well as they look, Bourget, who founded his Bike Works in 1994, has focused his energies on innovative chassis construction as a means of crafting different chopper designs. The T6 Low Blow rigid, for example, places a tuned, balanced, and blueprinted S&S/Delkron motor inside a frame built from dense, 1-1/2-inch chrome-moly tubing, twisted into an unusual rear section that places the riders just 19 inches from the pavement. More than just an eye-grabbing design, Bourget's frames feature CNC-machined engine mounts and oil-in-frame systems, eliminating the need for a separate lubricant tank. Bourget's performance leanings have resulted in choppers outfitted with dual chrome nitrous-oxide bottles mounted into his trademark stretched gas tanks, carrying on a tradition of fast, street-worthy choppers that dates back to the earliest drag-strip origins of the species.

Long live the longbike.

Paul Martinez

Index

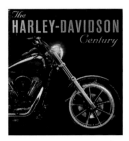
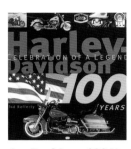

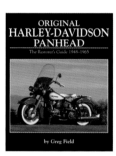